6th International Workshop for Computational Linguistics of Uralic Languages 2020

Wien, Austria
10 – 11 January 2020

ISBN: 978-1-7138-0863-3

Printed from e-media with permission by:

Curran Associates, Inc.
57 Morehouse Lane
Red Hook, NY 12571

Some format issues inherent in the e-media version may also appear in this print version.

Association for Computational Linguistics
209 N. Eighth Street
Stroudsburg, Pennsylvania 18360

Phone: 1-570-476-8006
Fax: 1-570-476-0860

acl@aclweb.org

Additional copies of this publication are available from:

Curran Associates, Inc.
57 Morehouse Lane
Red Hook, NY 12571 USA
Phone: 845-758-0400
Fax: 845-758-2633
Email: curran@proceedings.com
Web: www.proceedings.com

ACL SIGUR 2020

The Sixth International Workshop on Computational Linguistics for Uralic Languages

Proceedings of the Conference

January 10 — 11, 2020
Wien, Austria

Introduction

IWCLUL 2020 was held in Wien, Austria.

Organizers:

ACL SIGUR:
Tommi A. Pirinen, University of Hamburg
Francis M. Tyers, Indiana University Bloomington

Local Organizers:

Jeremy Bradley, University of Wien
Johannes Hirvonen, University of Wien

Program Committee:

Tommi A. Pirinen, University of Hamburg
Francis M. Tyers, Indiana University Bloomington
Jeremy Bradley, University of Vienna
Eszter Simon, Research Institute for Linguistics, Hungarian Academy of Sciences
Kadri Muischnek, University of Tartu
Michael Rießler, University of Eastern Finland
Filip Ginter, University of Turku
Timofey Arkhangelskiy, University of Hamburg / Alexander von Humboldt Foundation
Veronika Vincze, Research Group on Articial Intelligence, Hungarian Academy of Sciences
Roman Yangarber, University of Helsinki
Miikka Silfverberg, University of Helsinki

Invited Speaker:

Timofey Arkhangelskiy, University of Hamburg / Alexander von Humboldt Foundation

Table of Contents

Conference Program

Friday, January 10th, 2020

9:00–10:00 ***Registration***

10:00–10:15 ***Opening***

10:15–11:00 *Invited Talk: Timofey Arkhangelskiy*

11:00–11:30 ***Coffee break***

11:30–13:00 **Session 1**

11:30–12:00 *A pseudonymisation method for language documentation corpora: An experiment with spoken Komi*
Rogier Blokland, Niko Partanen and Michael Rießler

12:00–12:30 *Effort-value payoff in lemmatisation for Uralic languages*
Nick Howell, Maria Bibaeva and Francis M. Tyers

12:30–13:00 *On the questions in developing computational infrastructure for Komi-Permyak*
Jack Rueter, Niko Partanen and Larisa Ponomareva

13:00–14:00 ***Lunch***

Friday, January 10th, 2020 (continued)

14:00–15:00	**Session 2**
14:00–14:30	*On Editing Dictionaries for Uralic Languages in an Online Environment* Khalid Alnajjar, Mika Hämäläinen and Jack Rueter
14:30–15:00	*Towards a Speech Recognizer for Komi, an Endangered and Low-Resource Uralic Language* Nils Hjortnaes, Niko Partanen, Michael Rießler and Francis M. Tyers
15:00–15:30	***Coffee break***
15:30–17:00	**Session 3**
15:30–16:00	*Hunting for antiharmonic stems in Erzya* László Fejes
16:00–16:30	*apPILcation: an Android-based Tool for Learning Mansi* Gábor Bobály, Csilla Horváth and Veronika Vincze
16:30–17:00	***Closing***
17:00–18:30	***SIGUR business meeting***
20:00	***Dinner***

Saturday, January 11th, 2020

9:00–16:00 ***Tutorials***

A pseudonymisation method for language documentation corpora: An experiment with spoken Komi

Niko Partanen
University of Helsinki
Helsinki, Finland
niko.partanen@helsinki.fi

Rogier Blokland
Uppsala University
Uppsala, Sweden
rogier.blokland@moderna.uu.se

Michael Rießler
University of Eastern Finland
Joensuu, Finland
michael.riessler@uef.fi

Abstract

This article introduces a novel and creative application of the Constraint Grammar formalism, by presenting an automated method for pseudonymising a Zyrian Komi spoken language corpus in an effective, reliable and scalable manner. The method is intended to be used to minimize various kinds of personal information found in the corpus in order to make spoken language data available while preventing the spread of sensitive personal data about the recorded informants or other persons mentioned in the texts. In our implementation, a Constraint Grammar based pseudonymisation tool is used as an automatically applied shallow layer that derives from the original corpus data a version which can be shared for open research use.

Teesiq

Seo artikli tutvustas vahtsõt ja loovat piirdmiisi grammatiga (PG) formalismõ pruuk´mist. Taas om metod´, kon PG pruugitas tuusjaos, et süräkomi kõnõldu keele korpusõ lindistuisi saassiq tegüsähe, kimmähe ja kontrol´misõvõimalusõga vaŕonim miga käkkiq. Seo metod´ om tett, et korpusõn saassiq kõnõlõjidõ andmit nii pall´o vähembäs võttaq, ku või, ja et tulõmit saassiq kergehe käsilde kontrolliq. Mi plaani perrä pruugitas taad ku automaatsõt kihti, miä tege korpusõ säändses, et taad või kergehe uuŕmisõ jaos jakaq.

1 Introduction

The research presented in this paper is predominantly relevant for documentary linguistics, aiming at the creation of a "lasting multipurpose record of a language" (Himmelmann, 2006, 1), while applying a computational linguistic approach to an endangered Uralic language. Specifically, we are developing an automated method for pseudonymising the textual representation of a spoken language corpus in order to make the corpus data publishable while 1) preventing the spread of sensitive personal data, 2) overcome manual work in the process to the extent possible, and 3) keeping the pseudonymised data as one – more openly distributed – version of the original – and less openly distributed – data, rather than destroying the latter by overwriting or cutting away parts of them.

To our knowledge, this is a novel approach in documentary linguistics, which so far seems to rely mostly on manual methods for pseudonymising (or anonymising) corpus data or bypasses the problem, typically by generally applying very restrict access protocols to corpus data preventing them from being openly published.

Computational linguistic projects aiming at corpus building for endangered languages, on the other hand, are rarely faced the problem of personal data protection because their corpora typically originate from written texts, which either are openly available to begin with or for which access rights have been cleared before the work with corpus building starts. Different from written-language data, corpora resulting from fieldwork-based spoken-language documentation invariably contain large amounts and various kinds of personal data. The reason for this is that documentary linguists transcribe authentic speech samples meant to be re-used in multidisciplinary research beyond structural linguistics.

Proceedings of the 6th International Workshop on Computational Linguistics of Uralic Languages, pages 1–8
Wien, Austria, January 10 — 11, 2020. © 2020 Association for Computational Linguistics
https://doi.org/10.18653/v1/FIXME

Typically, recordings are done with members of small communities, where most individuals know each other, and common topics include oral histories about places, persons or events inevitably including personal information about the informants itself or other individuals.

Although the recorded speaker's informed consent to further processing and re-using the speech sample needs to be at hand in any case, fieldwork-based recordings nearly always include information which should not be made entirely openly available. Simultaneously, it is in the natural interest of documentary linguistics to make as many materials as widely available as possible. The approach discussed in this paper consequently attempts to find a suitable middle way in presenting our Zyrian Komi corpus to a wider audience, in this case mainly researchers such as linguists and anthropologists, whilst ensuring that the privacy of individual speakers is respected and the risk of miss-using personal data can be excluded.

Best practice recommendations related to the problem of personal data protection in Open Science are currently evolving (cf. Seyfeddinipur et al., 2019), although relevant issues have been under discussion for a while already in the context of in Documentary Linguistics. The conventions and technical solutions described on this study have been developed in a specific situation, where the goal has been to publish and archive the corpus in the Language Bank of Finland (Blokland et al., 2020), and can hopefully contribute to solving at least some of the many challenges still remaining open.

Since GDPR-related[1] research practices are still evolving in Finland and there are as yet no clear guidelines, it is currently problematic to make audiovisual research materials containing identifiable personal information available. As there are fewer limitations when the material is anonymised or pseudonymised, we have explored this as a solution: a version of a corpus that does not contain identifiable personal information can be openly shared much more easily. The current approach we are considering is to share the current corpus with academic users through the Korp interface (Ahlberg et al., 2013) under so-called ACA conditions. This ensures that the users are authenticated as members of the academic community, and their identity is known. At this level, however, they can only access the versions that have passed through the pseudonymisation system described in this paper. We refer to this method as pseudonymisation, since the actual identity information is not discarded permanently from existence. We just derive a version where the personal data is minimised, and provide that to one particular user group.

We think this approach can be a satisfactory middle way to make the data accessible to the scientific community without needlessly revealing the personal information of individual speakers. We aim, however, to make the complete corpus available for research use with a specific application procedure, as is common with language documentation corpora in other archives.

These methods to share the corpora primarily serve academic users in Europe, but not the community itself, and to resolve this issue our colleagues from the community have also made a selection of the corpus available as a 'community edition' at a website videocorpora.ru[2], which is maintained and curated by FU-Lab (the Finno-Ugric Laboratory for the Support of Electronic Representation of Regional Languages in Syktyvkar, Russia). This, however, though trilingual (Zyrian Komi, Russian, English), is designed mainly from the point of view of and for community members, containing edited video versions aimed at an uncomplicated user experience, and does not (and is not primarily supposed to) satisfy the needs of many academic users.

In order to reliably pseudonymise the transcriptions in a version of the corpus aimed at research use we have developed a workflow that uses existing rule-based NLP for Zyrian Komi. The approach consists of performing an analysis on all running text, with various strategies to manipulate and filter out proper nouns, such as person names and toponyms. This allows us to keep some of the naturalness of the running text, while removing and changing easily identifiable content. Another benefit of our approach is that it lets us show which recordings contain which types of personal information.

Our method uses Finite-State Morphology (henceforth FST), specifically HFST (Lindén et al., 2009), and Constraint Grammar (henceforth CG) (Karlsson, 1990; Karlsson et al., 2011), specifically the CG-3 version (Bick and Didriksen, 2015), and is applied to the corpus using a uralicNLP Python package (Hämäläinen, 2019). The use of rule-based NLP methods is, in our opinion, highly desirable in this context as we can thus

[1]The General Data Protection Regulation (EU) 2016/679

[2]http://videocorpora.ru

carefully control the entire process, and be certain about the achieved result. Although we benefit from the existence of a highly advanced Komi morphological analyser (Rueter, 2000), we believe that this approach could also be applicable to other language documentation projects. In principle the analyser used for such projects would only need a very small lexicon containing those items to be pseudonymised, which could be very easily connected to the project's internal metadata.

2 Problem description

Much has been written on the problems with regard to the role of the linguistic consultants in language documentation, especially with regard to ethics and the acknowledgement of their role (see e.g. Rice, 2006; O'Meara and Good, 2010; Chelliah and Willem, 2010, 139–159; Dobrin and Berson, 2011; Bowern, 2015, 171–175). This may refer to making their identity known or not in publications, corpora and other sources, though acknowledging their role in the material collected, whether or not they wish to be overtly acknowledged by name, should in any case be done. As our aim is to share material as openly as possible we avoided collecting sensitive and personal information that could potentially be harmful for the individuals and communities when building our documentary corpus, and focused primarily on narratives that document local culture and history. Unfortunately, the current interpretations of EU legislation still leave some unclarity as to how questions of personal data in our recordings should be addressed.

Our research has been carried out in close cooperation with Zyrian Komi communities and native organisations, and we have made significant effort to ensure that our work is both accepted by the community and that the relevant materials are also available to community members. However, as e.g. Dorian (2010, 181) points out, consultants may not always fully grasp what exactly linguists plan on doing with the material they collect. Thereby we have to consider our own responsibility, independent of the informed consent provided by our language informants. We have to ensure that the ways the material is released to the public are appropriate.

The problem may be summarised such that even though we see no issues at the moment in sharing the complete dataset with the community, which we have already done in various ways (whilst taking into account the community's needs), and will also share it with researchers, most likely through a permission request with a description of intended use, it is currently not possible to share it entirely openly with the general public, as this would permanently expose community members' personal information. However, this kind of very formal and restricted method of distribution certainly hinders the active research use of the corpus, which is also something we do not want to happen. Thereby providing a pseudonymised version for the research use seems like a good alternative and something worth investigating further. When the pseudonymised version is available after an academically affiliated login in Korp, it is simple to familiarise oneself with the corpus to decide whether the complete dataset is needed for planned research. This also minimises the unnecessary redistribution of the entire corpus, as individuals do not need to access the complete dataset to evaluate its usability. In the same vein, with this information we can also create derived datasets that can be used in different experiments, but contain only minimal amount of personal data.

3 Method

The semantic tags that associate proper nouns in the Komi morphological analyser are: `Sem/Mal` (for a male forename), `Sem/Fem` (female forename), `Sem/Patr-Mal`, `Sem/Patr-Fem` (patronym), `Sem/Sur`, `Sem/Sur-Mal`, `Sem/Sur-Fem` (surname) and `Sem/Plc` (toponym). In addition to proper nouns numerals need specific attention, especially in constructions that are dates or years. Potentially, all tokens in the corpus tagged for one of these semantic categories contain information that either directly reveals the identity of individuals or information that can be easily used for revealing the identity of individuals when combined in combination with other data. The relevant identities can concern the recorded speaker(s) themselves (for instance the own name, names of parents and other relatives, or the place or date of birth) or they concern other individuals to which the recorded speaker is referring to. At the same time, however, spoken recordings contain names of places that are so large and general that they can be mentioned without in fact conveying a great deal of personal information. For example, cities such as Syktyvkar and Moscow have populations large enough such that identifying a person is usually not possible. The same is true for large bodies of water such as the rivers Izhma or Pechora, or mountain ranges like Ural mountains – they span so many localities that they do not actually identify any of them. All these larger entities are treated through the method presented in Section 3.1. However, for very small settlements it is important to be more careful, as some locations only consist of individual houses, and speakers can thereby be identified more easily than would usually be the case. Example 1, which is taken from the introductory part of a personal interview, clearly illustrates how an individual utterance can contain different types of identifiable personal information, of which some are larger entities, i.e. the capital of the Komi Republic Syktyvkar, that can remain unmodified.

(1) Менӧ шуӧны Александр, ме ола Вертепын, велӧдчи Сыктывкарын.

menə	*ʃu-əni*	*aʎeksandr,*	*me*
1SG.ACC	call-3PL.PRS	Aleksander	1SG
_	_	Sem/Mal	_

ol-a	*vertep-ɨn,*	*veləɕ:-i*
live-1SG.PRS	Vertep-INE	study-1SG.PST
_	Sem/Plc	_

sɨktɨvkar-ɨn
Syktyvkar-INE
Sem/Plc

'My name is Aleksander, I live in Vertep, I studied in Syktyvkar.'

We can therefore construct a list of major settlements that occur in our corpus, and allow those to pass unchanged through our pseudonymisation system. This is necessary, as the analyser would otherwise mark all places with the tag Sem/Plc. With regard to smaller localities, however, we have two options: 1) either mark them with an empty placeholder, or 2) replace the value with a specific "standard village". At the moment we have opted to use empty placeholders, although there are various options that should be considered. Example 1 illustrates how, using this logic, we can distinguish large localities of the type Syktyvkar from small ones such as Vertep.

Since the full name of each person we have worked with is included in our metadata database, it has been easy to evaluate whether all names are present in the Komi FST. Similarly, our metadata includes all names of recording locations, places of residence and places of birth. In practice, however, there are more place names mentioned in the narratives than those present in the metadata database, as the information in the database has originally been collected from those same interviews that were recorded and transcribed, i.e. the metadata referring to e.g. place names is limited to actual locations where people were born or lived or where recordings where made; place names merely mentioned in speech (like 'I visited Bangkok') have not been specially listed anywhere in our material. The work presented here is in principle one path toward constructing a more structured database of locations present in the corpus, which could be of high relevance for various types of linguistic and non-linguistic research using our data.

Another data type that potentially contains information sensitive to personal identities consists of dates. In the case of small local populations this can be true even for incomplete dates, i.e. indicating only the month of a year or even the year alone. Example 2 illustrates how this kind of information could be present in the corpus.

There is a tendency for such numbers to occur in formulaic expressions, especially as direct replies to questions about the age and such properties. In this kind of situation, when the numbers are pronounced in a very literary manner and are all in Komi, it is relatively easy to identify such segments. For instance, we can write a CG rule that targets sequences that contain the word for 'year' and a preceding sequence of numerals. Another way to target these segments would be to look into them as replies to questions where this content is asked. This would take advantage of the conversationality of the recordings.

However, there are particular challenges in those instances where the numbers are non-standard or in Russian, such as *пятого* 'fifth' in Example 2:

(2) Но ме рӧдитчи пятого декабря сюрс ӧкмыссё квайтымын витед воын.

no	*me*	*rədiɕɕ-i*	*pʲatovo*
well	1SG	be_born-1SG.PST	5th
_	_	_	Num/Card

dʲekabrʲa	*ɕurɕ*	*əkmɨsɕo*
December	1000	900
_	Num/Ord	Num/Ord

kvajtɨmɨn	*vit-ed*	*vo-ɨn*
60	5-CARD	year-INE
Num/Ord	Num/Card	_

'Well, I was born on the 5.12.1965'

The problem here is essentially that parts of the sentence are in Russian. Therefore, we cannot analyse it with the Komi analyser alone. The method has not yet been fully implemented for multilingual data, as processing such material contains numerous mixed forms and other problems. The process currently planned is to pass all unrecognised words through a Russian analyser, which, however, would also demand some consistency in tagging schemes used across these analysers. Cross-linguistic annotation schemes cannot always be straightforwardly matched (see discussion in Rueter and Partanen, 2019), but for a number of tasks any improvement here is very beneficial.

3.1 Implementation logic

Since CG does not allow us to modify the transcribed words directly, our method has been implemented through CG rules that add additional tags and prefixes to the available FST readings. For example, basic semantic tags do not need to be edited at this point, with the exception of locations that we want to keep, as described above. The CG rule that adds an additional tag for locations sufficiently large to be kept intact is very simple:

Keeping large toponyms

```
SUBSTITUTE:keep-large-places
(Sem/Plc) (Sem/LargePlc)
TARGET LARGE-PLACES ;
```

When this rule is applied, the later processing steps do not apply to locations marked with the *Sem/LargePlc* tag.

This rule depends on the list LARGE-PLACES which holds information about all the larger towns and settlements that we want to retain in the pseudonymised corpus. The list is manually compiled and contains some tens of generic large locations in Russia and elsewhere, among them common holiday destinations. It could be possible, however, to also connect this list to common open databases such as Wikidata,[3] in order to let the rule automatically apply to all settlements that have a population, for instance, over half a million. This, however, would move from the current direction where the rules are edited based on our own observations and thorough knowledge of the material, although the changes are implemented through the CG.

For removing birthday data we have experimented with a set of rules that are specific for that context. The rule **Explicit years** below briefly illustrates this logic, although the actual implementation is slightly more complicated with more word order variation included.

Explicit years

```
ADD:find-dates-years (Date)
TARGET (Num) OR (Ord)
((1* ("во")) OR (1* ("год"))) ;

ADD:find-dates-born (DateBirth)
TARGET (Num) OR (Ord)
((-1* ("чужны"))
OR (-1* ("рӧдитчывны"))
OR (-1*("рӧдитчыны"))) ;
```

Such contextual rules are useful as we can be relatively sure that this date is a date of birth, which is then tagged accordingly. There are, however, so many instances of dates that are without contiguous context that we have decided to use a rule that removes all years and dates. However, having the explicit information available about possible dates of birth in the corpus is very important and increases the accountability of the corpus creators.

All in all the system is relatively simple, consisting of some tens of CG rules. The actual removal of the sensitive tokens is done by a script reading the tagset that is specifically inserted through our rules. The script removes the actual tokens while leaving in the resulting pseudonymised corpus a placeholder-token, including the belonging morphosyntactic tags coming from the FST analyser.

The process is implemented as Python functions that are currently used as a part in the script pipeline that convert from the original corpus data in XML format used by ELAN into VRT format needed by Korp. There is, however, no reason why the same methods could not be adapted to other environments not working with ELAN or Korp.

The whole pipeline has been published in Zenodo (Partanen, 2019) and GitHub[4].

4 Evaluation

The quality of the system was evaluated with one pass through the complete corpus, and another more qualitative examination of one individual recording

[3]https://www.wikidata.org

[4]https://github.com/langdoc/langdoc-pseudonymization

of five speakers. This gives a relatively good impression of the accuracy and also the usability of the method. If the resulting text is unusable with too many omitted sections it is clear that the method is not of particular use for researchers.

In the complete corpus currently 2% of all tokens get marked as being possible proper names of persons, places or dates. During evaluation we also found that it was necessary to adjust the system so that both Russian and Komi language versions of the names of settlements are included in the analyser, as the speakers may use both. Some toponyms for smaller places, for instance *Мохча*, were missing from the analyser, as were some less-used patronyms, for instance *Парфёнович* and *Арсентьевна*. Adding these is, obviously, a trivial task. However, looking also at the Russian analyser benefits the infrastructure at large, as these same names occur in various languages spoken in Russia.

Interestingly, our evaluation run revealed also situations where the system *en passant* removes ambiguously tagged content. One such example is the lemma *Бура*, which could be analysed as a surname or as an adverb. However, to our knowledge it is only used as an adverb with the meaning 'well' and never as a surname. The problem is related to various names that are foreign in cultural context in Komi, but in theory could be foreign names. Also several common Russian words have a potential surname reading, which by our evaluation is not relevant in our corpus. These are, for example, *Горячий*, *Ден* and *Готов*. We have relaxed the the system with additional rules to ignore such cases, but with careful consideration only.

One culturally important feature of our method is that it can correctly detect native Komi names, such as the multi-word *Пась Коля*. Among surnames a category of individuals who are so well known that they do not need to be removed is still under consideration. With some names this is clear, for instance, all tokens *Вихман* 'Wichmann' occurring in the corpus refer to the Finnish researcher Yrjö Wichmann. Similarly, names such as 'Jesus' or 'Lenin' are kept, as these names are not used as a given name or nick name in our cultural context. Other surnames, such as *Лыткин* 'Lytkin', may either refer to the well known Komi researcher Vasily Lytkin or other persons with the same name. Therefore, this part of the system needs refinement.

One benefit of using an orthographic transcription system for a spoken-language corpus (instead of phonemic transcription, cf. Blokland et al., 2015; Gerstenberger et al., 2016) is that orthographically proper nouns are consistently written with initial uppercase. Their parsing and verification for our pseudonymisation system is therefore an easy process. Our evaluation run revealed a list of approximately 7000 tokens with initial uppercase letters, that were not being recognised by the analyser yet. It has been possible to go through this list manually while collecting the forms. As these were primarily items missing from the lexicon, their inclusion was simple. Note also that since our field recordings have been carried out in a limited number of communities, the same toponyms are repeated in different recordings. All work with including these missing names in the analyser's lexicon files rapidly improves the performance of the analyser overall. All in all, our examination resulted in approximately 250 new lemmas being added into the lexicon files of the Komi morphological analyser.

In one particular category of toponyms, names derive from common nouns designating landscape features, such as *Ді* /di/ 'island' and *Ёль* /joʎ/ 'stream'. In such instances the pseudonymisation is done only when they are written with capital letter and are in singular. Although this rule overgeneralises a few relevant common nouns in sentence initial position, it seems to handle this problem sufficiently. Some concepts are, however, so generic that to our knowledge they do not refer uniquely to individual settlements specifically, i.e. *Яг* /jag/ 'forest', *Курья* /kurja/ 'bay' and *Катыд* /katɨd/ 'downstream'. The proper noun reading is left at place when the form is written in lower case, but does not have any other possible interpretations. This is against our transcription conventions, but it is beneficial that the system has some robustness for such instances where the spelling is by mistake deviating from our guidelines.

The evaluation of all tokens marked in the entire corpus as potentially containing personal information revealed that out of 8000 pseudonymised tokens only 4% were mistakenly removed. If we would had pseudonymised all items, which are semantically tagged as proper names or dates, without implementing further rules as described above, the ratio of mistakenly removed forms would had been almost 50% of the tagged ones. This is so primarily because very high frequency words such as *Из* /iz/ 'stone; Ural mountain; negation verb form' and *Коми* /komi/ 'Komi (Republic); Komi (an ethnic group, a language)' would had been tagged for pseudonymisation and removed by the script as well. This illustrates well, that such a task as writing rules for pseudonymisation can only be done with careful understanding of the data and its cultural context. The forms that cannot be proper nouns under any circumstances have been added to a separate list. There is always the possibility to edit such instances also at the level of the analyser itself.

5 Conclusion & Further work

Later evaluation should be linked to explicit tests that demonstrate that the rules are working under the desired conditions. However, already now the pipeline proposed in this paper has proven itself to be highly effective for the pseudonymisation of a large spoken-language corpus resulting from fieldwork recordings of an endangered language. The specific merits of this system are that it is easy to extend, and through rule-based implementation its precision can be very reliably evaluated and adjusted.

One possible, and already planned, utilization for our method is the selection of sentences that can be included into dictionaries as examples. There is a general need to display in different web interfaces spoken language sentences that illustrate how a word is used, and through our method we could automatise the task to select example sentences. This could be combined into modern dictionary interfaces such as those discussed by Rueter et al. (2017) and Hämäläinen and Rueter (2018).

We have described a method that is effective, reliable, and meets a concrete need in corpus data processing. We have also presented a novel and creative application for Constraint Grammar. We want to stress that besides removing or editing the marked personal information this method could also be used to evaluate how much of this kind of information individual transcriptions contain, thereby providing rough metrics about their level of sensitivity.

Since no anonymization or pseudonymisation method is perfectly reliable, the materials cannot be made entirely available without further manual verification. We believe, however, that the results we have achieved reach a level that does allow relatively open distribution with only basic user authentication, for example, within an academic research context. As the system described contains many changing elements: Komi FST, CG and the corpus itself, testing and refinement will necessarily continue.

Acknowledgments

The authors of this paper collaborate within the project "Language Documentation meets Language Technology: The Next Step in the Description of Komi", funded by the Kone Foundation, Finland. Special thanks to the University of Helsinki for funding Niko Partanen's travel.

Thanks to Jack Rueter for his valuable and continuous work on the computational description of Komi, and to Marina Fedina's team at FU-Lab in Syktyvkar for their ongoing efforts in building Komi language resources and language technology.

References

Malin Ahlberg, Lars Borin, Markus Forsberg, Martin Hammarstedt, Leif-Jöran Olsson, Olof Olsson, Johan Roxendal, and Jonatan Uppström. 2013. Korp and Karp–a bestiary of language resources: the research infrastructure of Språkbanken. In *Proceedings of the 19th Nordic Conference of Computational Linguistics (NODALIDA 2013)*, pages 429–433.

Eckhard Bick and Tino Didriksen. 2015. Cg-3—beyond classical constraint grammar. In *Proceedings of the 20th Nordic conference of computational linguistics, NODALIDA 2015, May 11-13, 2015, Vilnius, Lithuania*, 109, pages 31–39. Linköping University Electronic Press.

Rogier Blokland, Marina Fedina, Niko Partanen, and Michael Rießler. 2020. Spoken Komi Corpus. The Language Bank of Finland version.

Rogier Blokland, Ciprian Gerstenberger, Marina Fedina, Niko Partanen, Michael Rießler, and Joshua Wilbur. 2015. Language documentation meets language technology. In *First International Workshop on Computational Linguistics for Uralic Languages, 16th January, 2015, Tromsø, Norway*, number 2015:2 in Septentrio Conference Series, pages 8–18. The University Library of Tromsø.

Claire Bowern. 2015. *Linguistic fieldwork: A practical guide*. Springer.

Shobhana L Chelliah and Jules Willem. 2010. *Handbook of descriptive linguistic fieldwork*. Springer Science & Business Media.

Lise M Dobrin and Joshua Berson. 2011. Speakers and language documentation. In *The Cambridge handbook of endangered languages*, pages 187–211. Cambridge University Press.

Nancy C Dorian. 2010. Documentation and responsibility. *Language & Communication*, 30(3):179–185.

Ciprian Gerstenberger, Niko Partanen, Michael Rießler, and Joshua Wilbur. 2016. Utilizing language technology in the documentation of endangered Uralic languages. 4:29–47.

Mika Hämäläinen and Jack Rueter. 2018. Advances in synchronized XML-MediaWiki dictionary development in the context of endangered Uralic languages. In *Proceedings of the eighteenth EURALEX international congress*, pages 967–978.

Nikolaus Himmelmann. 2006. Language documentation. In Jost Gippert, Ulrike Mosel, and Nikolaus Himmelmann, editors, *Essentials of Language Documentation*, number 178 in Trends in Linguistics. Studies and Monographs, pages 1–30. Mouton de Gruyter.

Mika Hämäläinen. 2019. UralicNLP: An NLP library for Uralic languages. *Journal of Open Source Software*, 4(37):1345.

Fred Karlsson. 1990. Constraint grammar as a framework for parsing running text. In *COLNG 1990 Volume 3: Papers presented to the 13th International Conference on Computational Linguistics*.

Fred Karlsson, Atro Voutilainen, Juha Heikkilae, and Arto Anttila. 2011. *Constraint Grammar: a language-independent system for parsing unrestricted text*, volume 4. Walter de Gruyter.

Krister Lindén, Miikka Silfverberg, and Tommi Pirinen. 2009. Hfst tools for morphology–an efficient open-source package for construction of morphological analyzers. In *International Workshop on Systems and Frameworks for Computational Morphology*, pages 28–47. Springer.

Carolyn O'Meara and Jeff Good. 2010. Ethical issues in legacy language resources. *Language & Communication*, 30(3):162–170.

Niko Partanen. 2019. langdoc/langdoc-pseudonymization: Language documentation corpus pseudonymization method.

Keren Rice. 2006. Ethical issues in linguistic fieldwork: An overview. *Journal of Academic Ethics*, 4(1-4):123–155.

Jack Rueter and Niko Partanen. 2019. Survey of Uralic Universal Dependencies development. In *Workshop on Universal Dependencies*, page 78. Association for Computational Linguistics.

Jack M. Rueter. 2000. Хельсинкиса университетын кыв туялысь Ижкарын перымса симпозиум вылын лыддьӧмтор. In *Пермистика 6 (Proceedings of Permistika 6 conference)*, pages 154–158.

Jack Michael Rueter, Mika Kalevi Hämäläinen, et al. 2017. Synchronized Mediawiki based analyzer dictionary development. In *3rd International Workshop for Computational Linguistics of Uralic Languages Proceedings of the Workshop*. Association for Computational Linguistics.

Mandana Seyfeddinipur, Felix Ameka, Lissant Bolton, Jonathan Blumtritt, Brian Carpenter, Hilaria Cruz, Sebastian Drude, Patience L Epps, Vera Ferreira, Ana Vilacy Galucio, et al. 2019. Public access to research data in language documentation: Challenges and possible strategies. *Language Documentation and Conservation*, 13:545–563.

Effort versus performance tradeoff in Uralic lemmatisers

Nicholas Howell and **Maria Bibaeva**
National Research University Higher School of Economics, Moscow, Russia

Francis M. Tyers
National Research University Higher School of Economics, Moscow, Russia
Indiana University, Bloomington, IN, United States

Abstract

Lemmatisers in Uralic languages are required for dictionary lookup, an important task for language learners. We explore how to decide which of the rule-based and unsupervised categories is more efficient to invest in. We present a comparison of rule-based and unsupervised lemmatisers, derived from the Giellatekno finite-state morphology project and the Morfessor surface segmenter trained on Wikipedia, respectively. The comparison spanned six Uralic languages, from relatively high-resource (Finnish) to extremely low-resource (Uralic languages of Russia). Performance is measured by dictionary lookup and vocabulary reduction tasks on the Wikipedia corpora. Linguistic input was quantified, for rule-based as quantity of source code and state machine complexity, and for unsupervised as the size of the training corpus; these are normalised against Finnish. Most languages show performance improving with linguistic input. Future work will produce quantitative estimates for the relationship between corpus size, ruleset size, and lemmatisation performance.

Abstract

Uralilaisten kielten sanakirjahakuihin tarvitaan lemmatisoijia, jotka tulevat tarpeeseen kielenoppijan etsiessä sanan perusmuotoa. Tutkimme miten päästään selville sääntöpohjaisten ja ohjastamattomien lemmatisoijien luokittelun tehokkuudesta ja mihin pitää sijoittaa lisää työtä. Esittelemme vertailun Giellateknon äärellistilaisen morfologian projektista derivoiduista sääntöpohjaisista lemmatisoijista sekä Morfessor -pintasegmentoijaprojektin ohjastamattomista lemmatisoijista, jotka on opetettu Wikipedia-aineistoilla. Vertailu koskee kuutta uralilaista kieltä, joista suomi edustaa suhteellisen suuriresurssista kieltä ja Venäjän uralilaiset kielet edustavat erityisen vähäresurssisia kieliä. Suoritusta mitataan sanakirjahakuja sanastovähentämistehtävillä Wikipediakorpuksilla. Kielellistä syötettä kvantifioitiin siten, että lähdekoodi- ja äärellistilakoneen monipuolisuutta pidettiin sääntöpohjaisten lemmatisoijien mittana, ja ohjastamattomien lemmatisoijien mittana pidettiin opetuskorpusta. Näiden molempien mittausta normalisoitiin suomen arvoilla. Valtaosa kielistä näyttää suoriutuvan tehtävästä paranevalla tavalla sitä mukaa, kun kielellistä syötettä lisätään. Tulevassa työssä tehdään kvantitatiivisia arviointeja korpuskoon, säännöstösuuruuden ja lemmatisointisuorituksen välisistä suhteista.

1 Introduction

Lemmatisation is the process of deinflecting a word (the *surface form*) to obtain a normalised, grammatically "neutral" form, called the *lemma*.

A related task is **stemming**, the process of removing affix morphemes from a word, reducing it to the intersection of all surface forms of the same lemma.

These two operations have finer (meaning more informative) variants: morphological analysis (producing the lemma plus list of morphological tags) and surface segmentation (producing the stem plus list of affixes). Still, a given surface form may have several possible analyses and several possible segmentations.

Uralic languages are highly agglutinative, that is, inflection is often performed by appending suffixes to the lemma. For such languages, stemming and lemmatisation agree, allowing one dimension of comparison between morphological analysers and surface segmenters.

Such agglutinative languages typically do not have all surface forms listed in a dictionary; users wishing to look up a word must lemmatise before performing the lookup. Software tools (Johnson et al., 2013) are being developed to combine the lemmatisation and lookup operations.

Further, most Uralic languages are low-resourced, meaning large corpora (necessary for the training of some analysers and segmenters) are not readily available. In such cases, software engineers, linguists and system designers must decide whether to invest effort in obtaining a large enough corpus for statistical methods or in writing rulesets for a rule-based system.

Proceedings of the 6th International Workshop on Computational Linguistics of Uralic Languages, pages 9–14
Wien, Austria, January 10 — 11, 2020.
https://doi.org/10.18653/v1/FIXME

In this article we explore this trade-off, comparing rule-based and statistical stemmers across several Uralic languages (with varying levels of resources), using a number of proxies for "model effort".

For rule-based systems, we evaluate the Giellatekno (Moshagen et al., 2014) finite-state morphological transducers, exploring model effort through ruleset length, and number of states of the transducer.

For statistical systems, we evaluate Morfessor (Virpioja et al., 2013) surface segementer models along with training corpus size.

We hope to provide guidance on the question, "given an agglutinative language with a corpus of N words, how much effort might a rule-based analyser require to be better than a statistical segmenter at lemmatisation?"

1.1 Reading Guide

The most interesting results of this work are the figures shown in Section 5.4, where effort proxies are plotted against several measures of performance (normalised against Finnish). The efficient reader may wish to look at these first, looking up the various quantities afterwards.

For (brief) information on the languages involved, see Section 2; to read about the morphological analysers and statistical segmenters used, see Section 3.

Discussion and advisement on directions for future work conclude the article in Section 6. The entire project is reproducible, and will be made available before publication.

2 Languages

The languages used for the experiments in this paper are all of the Uralic group. These languages are typologically agglutinative with predominantly suffixing morphology. The following paragraphs give a brief introduction to each of the languages.

Finnish (ISO-639-3 `fin`) is the majority and official (together with Swedish) language of Finland. It is in the Finnic group of Uralic languages, and has an estimate of around 6 million speakers worldwide. The language, like other Uralic languages spoken in the more western regions of the language area has predominantly SVO word order and NP-internal agreement.

Komi-Zyrian (ISO-639-3 `kpv`; often simply referred to as Komi) is one of the major varieties of the Komi macrolanguage of the Permic group of Uralic languages. It is spoken by the Komi-Zyrians, the most populous ethnic subgroup of the Komi peoples in the Uralic regions of the Russian Federation. Komi languages are spoken by an estimated 220, 00 people, and are co-official with Russian in the Komi Republic and the Perm Krai territory of the Russian Federation.

Moksha (ISO-639-3 `mdf`) is one of the two Mordvinic languges, the other being Erzya; the two share co-official status with Russian in the Mordovia Republic of the Russian Federation. There are an estimated 2, 000 speakers of Moksha, and it is dominant in the Western part of Mordovia.

Meadow Mari (ISO-639-3 `mhr`, also known as Eastern Mari) is one of the minor languages of Russia belonging to the Finno-Volgaic group of the Uralic family. After Russian, it is the second-most spoken language of the Mari El Republic in the Russian Federation, and an estimated 500, 000 speakers globally. Meadow Mari is co-official with Hill Mari and Russian in the Mari El Republic.

Hill Mari (ISO-639-3 `mrj`; also known as Western Mari) is one of the minor languages of Russia belonging to the Finno-Volgaic group of the Uralic family, with an estimated 30, 000 speakers. It is closely related to Meadow Mari (ISO-639-3 `mhr`, also known as Eastern Mari, and Hill Mari is sometimes regarded as a dialect of Meadow Mari. Both languages are co-official with Russian in the Mari El Republic.

Erzya (ISO-639-3 `myv`) is one of the two Mordvinic languages, the other being Moksha, which are traditionally spoken in scattered villages throughout the Volga Region and former Russian Empire by well over a million in the beginning of the 20th century and down to approximately half a million according to the 2010 census. Together with Moksha and Russian, it shares co-official status in the Mordovia Republic of the Russian Federation.[1]

North Sámi (ISO-639-3 `sme`) belongs to the Samic branch of the Uralic languages. It is spoken in the Northern parts of Norway, Sweden and Finland by approximately 24.700 people, and it has, alongside the national language, some official status in the municipalities and counties where it is spoken. North Sámi speakers are bilingual in their mother tongue and in their respective national language, many also speak the neighbouring official language. It is primarily an SVO language with limited NP-internal agreement. Of all the languages studied it has the most complex phonological processes.

Udmurt (ISO-639-3 `udm`) is a Uralic language in the Permic subgroup spoken in the Volga area of the Russian Federation. It is co-official with Russian in the Republic of Udmurtia. As of 2010 it has around 340,000 native speakers.

Grammatically as with the other languages it is agglutinative, with 15 noun cases, seven of which are locative cases. It has two numbers, singular and plural and a series of possessive suffixes which decline for three persons and two numbers.

In terms of word order typology, the language is SOV, like many of the other Uralic languages of the Russian Federation. There are a number of grammars of the language in Russian and in English, e.g. Winkler (2001).

[1] `https://efo.revues.org/1829`

Table 1: Giellatekno bilingual dictionary sizes, in words.

Language	Lexemes
fin	19012
kpv	43362
mdf	28953
mhr	53134
mrj	6052
myv	15401
sme	17605
udm	19639

3 Lemmatisers

3.1 Giellatekno transducers

Giellatekno is a research group working on language technology for the Sámi languages. It is based in Tromsø, Norway and works primarily on rule-based language technology, particularly finite-state morphological descriptions and constraint grammars. In addition to the Sámi languages, their open-source infrastructure also contains software and data for many other Uralic languages.

In particular, Giellatekno has produced (Moshagen et al., 2014) finite-state transducers for morphological analysis of our chosen Uralic languages; we use these to extract lemmas from surface forms. When multiple lemmatisations are offered, the highest weight one is chosen. Unaccepted words are treated as already-lemmatised.

3.2 Morfessor

Morfessor (Virpioja et al., 2013) is a class of unsupervised and semi-supervised trainable surface segmentation algorithms; it attempts to find a minimal dictionary of morphemes. We use Wikipedia as training data for this model.

4 Evaluation

4.1 Dictionary task

The stemmers are applied to every word in the corpus, and the resulting stem is looked up in a dictionary. This mimics a user attempting to look up a highlighted word in a dictionary.

Bilingual dictionaries are taken from Giellatekno, with definitions in Russian, Finnish, English, or German. (The actual definitions are not used, just the presence of an entry; we take the union over all dictionaries.) Dictionary sizes are shown in Table 1.

As baseline we take the percentage of words in the corpus which are already in the dictionary. Both token and type counts provided.

4.2 Vocabulary reduction

We apply the lemmatisers to each word of the corpus, and measure the reduction in tokens and types. Lower diversity of post-lemmatisation tokens or types demonstrates that the lemmatiser is identifying more words as having the same lemma.

The distinction between token reduction and type reduction corresponds to a notion of "user experience": from the perspective of our tasks, correctly lemmatising a more frequent token is more important than a less frequent token.

4.3 Effort

The effort expended in producing a model is a subjective and qualitative measure; we claim only to provide coarse objective and quantitative proxies for this.

In the case of statistical methods, total effort (which would include the effort of developing the algorithm) is not important for our purposes: we are comparing the specialisation of a statistical method to a particular language with the development of a rule-based model. (Indeed, to fairly compare total effort of the technique, a completely different and perhaps more academic question, we would need to include the general development of rule-based methods.) Thus for statistical methods we include only the size of the corpus used to train the system. In our experiments, this corpus is Wikipedia, which we use (for better or worse) as a proxy for general availability of corpora in a given language on the internet.

For rule-based systems, we must find a measure of the effort. In this article our rule-based systems are all finite-state transducers, compiled from rulesets written by linguists. We choose two proxies for invested effort: the lines of code in all rulesets used in compiling the transducer, and the number of states of the transducer.

The former will count complex and simple rules the same, which the latter may provide insight into. Conversely, a highly powerful rule system may create a great number of states while being simple to write; in this case, the ruleset is a better proxy than the number of states.

4.4 Wikipedia

Wikipedia dumps from 20181201 are used as source corpus; the corpus is split into tokens at word boundaries and tokens which are not purely alphabetical are dropped. Corpus size in tokens, post-processing, is shown in Table 2.

Corpora were randomly divided into training (90% of the corpus) and testing subcorpora (10%); Morfessor models are produced with the training subcorpus, and lemmatiser evaluation is only with the test subcorpus.

5 Results

Our study involves treating the Uralic language as an independent variable; the six languages we consider here do not provide for a very large sample. We attempt to mitigate this by using both traditional and robust statistics; potential "outliers" can then be quantitatively identified. Thus for every mean and standard deviation seen, we will also present the *median* and the *median absolute deviation*.

Table 2: Wikipedia corpus size by language, in alphabetic words.

Language	Tokens	Types
fin	897867	276761
mrj	352521	51420
mhr	15159	6468
myv	11177	5107
sme	9442	6552
udm	7503	4308

For reference: suppose that $\{x_i\}_{i=1}^N$ is a finite set of numbers. If $\{y_i\}_{i=1}^N$ is the same collection, but sorted (so that $y_1 \leq y_2 \leq \cdots \leq y_N$), then the median is

$$\mathrm{med}\{x_i\} = \begin{cases} y_{N/2} & N \text{ is even} \\ \mathrm{mean}\{y_{(N\pm1)/2}\} & N \text{ is odd} \end{cases}$$

and the median absolute deviation (or for brevity, "median deviation") is

$$\mathrm{mad}\{x_i\} = \mathrm{med}\left\{|x_i - \mathrm{med}\, x_i|\right\}.$$

When we quote means, we will write them as $\mu \pm \sigma$ where μ is the mean and σ the standard deviation of the data. Similarly, for medians we will write $m \pm d$ where m is the median and d the median deviation.

Data with potential outliers can be identified by comparing the median/median deviation and the mean/standard deviation: if they are significantly different (for example, the mean is much further than one standard deviation away from the median, or the median deviation is much smaller than the standard deviation), then attention is likely warranted.

5.1 Dictionary lookup

Results of the dictionary lookup are presented in Table 3.

Cursory inspection shows that while the Giellatekno model for Finnish slightly out-performs the Wikipedia Morfessor model, on average Morfessor provides not only the greatest improvement in token lookup performance (average/median improvement of $1.6/1.5$ versus Giellatekno's $1.4/1.3$), but also more consistent (standard/median deviation of $0.3/0.1$ versus $0.4/0.3$).

We see some limitations in the Morfessor model when projecting to type lookup performance: the value of Morfessor on type lookup is essentially random, hurting as often and as much as it helps: mean and median improvement factors are both 1.0. Compare with Giellatekno, where improvement mean and median are at least one deviation above baseline. We suggest this disparity could be due to our Morfessor model over-stemming rare words, and successfully stemming common words.

5.2 Vocabulary reduction

Vocabulary reduction results are presented in Table 4.

Generally, we see that Morfessor is much more aggressively reducing the vocabulary: average Morfessor reduction is 9% versus Giellatekno's 15%; here North Sámi and Finnish again stand out with Morfessor reducing to 7.2% and 6.5% respectively. Compare with Hill Mari, where reduction is to a mere 11%.

While the performance of Giellatekno is much less dramatic, we still notice that North Sámi and Hill Mari are more than a standard deviation, or more than two median deviations, away from the mean performance. Otherwise, the clustering is fairly tight, with all languages besides North Sámi and Hill Mari within one standard deviation and 1.5 median deviations.

The analysis above shows that our data are affected by outlier models; which of the two measures is nominally more representative of the overall performance landscape could be demonstrated through an increase of sample size, i.e., increasing the number of languages surveyed.

5.3 Effort

The effort quantification is presented in Table 5. Transducer source code complexity, measured in number of transducer states per line of source code, is presented in Table 6. Note that comments are included as part of the "source code"; we consider, for example, explanation of how the code works to count as some of the effort behind the development of the transducer.

Some immediate observations: among the Uralic languages studied here, Finnish is high-resource, but not overwhelmingly: North Sámi compares for transducer size (in number of states), at nearly 2.5 times the median. While Meadow Mari actually has a comparable amount of transducer source code (1.8 million lines of code, about 80% the size of the Finnish transducer), its transducer code is extremely low complexity; see Table 6. Finnish Wikipedia is approximately 2.5 times larger than the next largest, Hill Mari, and nearly 7 times larger than the median; under our assumption, this would indicate that Finnish written material is also much more accessible on the internet than our other Uralic languages.

Among Giellatekno models, Hill Mari transducer is uniformly the lowest-resource of the Uralic languages studied, with very few lines of below-average complexity code written; contrast this with the Morfessor models, where Hill Mari has a respectable $350,000$ tokens. The lowest resource Morfessor model is Udmurt, with only $7,000$ tokens; the Udmurt Giellatekno model is also significantly below-average in resources.

While North Sámi has slightly below-median transducer source size, it has extremely high (eight deviations above median) state complexity, with more than one state for every two lines of code.

5.4 Analysis

See Figures 1, 2, and 3 for plots of effort normalised against Finnish versus performance. Plots are colored by language and marked by the effort quantification method. Note that since "lines of code" and "number of states" are two different measures of the same model,

Table 3: Results of the dictionary lookup task for no-op (NOOP), Morfessor (MF), and Giellatekno transducer (GT). A "hit" means a successful dictionary lookup. Percentage hits (tokens or types) is the percentage of tokens or types in the corpus for which the lemmatiser produces a dictionary word. The "no-op" (NOOP) lemmatiser takes the surface form as-is, and is used as baseline; the last two columns are percentage hits normalised by this.

Language	Lemmatiser	**Hits** (thous.)		**% Hits**		**Improvement**	
		tokens	**types**	**tokens**	**types**	**tokens**	**types**
`fin`	NOOP	10.2	2.55	11.0	5.0	-	-
`kpv`	NOOP	0.5	0.14	43.0	22.0	-	-
`mdf`	NOOP	2.1	0.75	32.0	19.0	-	-
`mhr`	NOOP	0.6	0.26	39.0	24.0	-	-
`mrj`	NOOP	5.4	0.76	15.0	6.0	-	-
`myv`	NOOP	0.4	0.13	38.0	19.0	-	-
`sme`	NOOP	0.1	0.08	15.0	10.0	-	-
`udm`	NOOP	0.2	0.14	31.0	22.0	-	-
average	NOOP	2.0 ± 3.0	0.6 ± 0.8	30.0 ± 10.0	16.0 ± 7.0	-	-
median	NOOP	0.5 ± 0.3	0.2 ± 0.09	32.0 ± 9.0	19.0 ± 4.0	-	-
`fin`	GT	19.1	3.0	21.0	6.0	1.9	1.2
`kpv`	GT	0.5	0.14	45.0	21.0	1.0	0.9
`mdf`	GT	3.9	1.08	61.0	27.0	1.9	1.4
`mhr`	GT	0.6	0.27	42.0	26.0	1.1	1.1
`mrj`	GT	8.3	0.88	23.0	7.0	1.5	1.1
`myv`	GT	0.4	0.17	38.0	24.0	1.0	1.3
`sme`	GT	0.3	0.14	29.0	17.0	2.0	1.7
`udm`	GT	0.3	0.16	35.0	25.0	1.1	1.1
average	GT	4.0 ± 6.0	0.7 ± 0.9	40.0 ± 10.0	19.0 ± 8.0	1.4 ± 0.4	1.2 ± 0.2
median	GT	0.6 ± 0.3	0.22 ± 0.08	36.0 ± 8.0	22.0 ± 4.0	1.3 ± 0.3	1.2 ± 0.1
`fin`	MORF	18.7	2.4	21.0	5.0	1.8	0.9
`kpv`	MORF	0.6	0.18	56.0	27.0	1.3	1.2
`mdf`	MORF	3.0	0.63	47.0	16.0	1.5	0.8
`mhr`	MORF	0.8	0.24	51.0	23.0	1.3	0.9
`mrj`	MORF	8.1	0.57	23.0	5.0	1.5	0.7
`myv`	MORF	0.6	0.13	49.0	19.0	1.3	1.0
`sme`	MORF	0.3	0.11	34.0	14.0	2.3	1.3
`udm`	MORF	0.3	0.15	45.0	24.0	1.4	1.1
average	MORF	4.0 ± 6.0	0.6 ± 0.7	40.0 ± 10.0	16.0 ± 8.0	1.6 ± 0.3	1.0 ± 0.2
median	MORF	0.7 ± 0.4	0.21 ± 0.09	46.0 ± 7.0	17.0 ± 6.0	1.5 ± 0.1	1.0 ± 0.1

Table 4: Vocabulary reduction results for no-op (NOOP), Morfessor (MF), and Giellatekno (GT) lemmatisers. The final column gives the reduction factor in vocabulary size: reduction of 1 corresponds to no reduction performed, while 0.01 corresponds to a 100-fold reduction in vocabulary (average of 100 types per lemma). Note that there is no constraint that the "lemmas" produced are dictionary words.

Lang.	Model	Lemmas (k)	% Red.
fin	NOOP	264.5	-
kpv	NOOP	4.7	-
mdf	NOOP	18.1	-
mhr	NOOP	6.3	-
mrj	NOOP	46.9	-
myv	NOOP	5.0	-
sme	NOOP	6.5	-
udm	NOOP	4.2	-
average	NOOP	45 ± 84	-
median	NOOP	6.4 ± 2.0	-
fin	GT	41.8	15.8
kpv	GT	0.6	13.6
mdf	GT	2.9	15.8
mhr	GT	1.0	16.6
mrj	GT	9.7	20.8
myv	GT	0.7	13.4
sme	GT	0.8	12.1
udm	GT	0.6	14.7
average	GT	7.3 ± 13	15.3 ± 2.5
median	GT	0.9 ± 0.3	15.2 ± 1.5
fin	MORF	17.1	6.5
kpv	MORF	0.4	9.1
mdf	MORF	1.8	9.9
mhr	MORF	0.6	9.9
mrj	MORF	5.2	11.1
myv	MORF	0.4	8.6
sme	MORF	0.5	7.2
udm	MORF	0.4	9.9
average	MORF	3.3 ± 5.4	9.0 ± 1.4
median	MORF	0.5 ± 0.1	9.5 ± 0.6

Table 5: Effort quantification; last column is normalized by Finnish. The group 'Mloc' refers to millions of lines of code in the Giellatekno transducer source, including `lexc`, `xfst`, regular expression, constrain grammar, and `twol` code. The group 'kst' is the number (in thousands) of states in the Giellatekno transducer, and 'ktok' is the number (in thousands) of tokens in the Morfessor training corpus. The final column normalises against Finnish.

Lang.	Model	Effort	Quan.	% fin
fin	GT	kst	440	100
kpv	GT	kst	150	35
mdf	GT	kst	60	13
mhr	GT	kst	80	17
mrj	GT	kst	50	11
myv	GT	kst	110	25
sme	GT	kst	540	122
udm	GT	kst	60	15
avg.	GT	kst	190 ± 180	40 ± 40
med.	GT	kst	90 ± 40	20 ± 9
fin	GT	Mloc	2.3	100.0
kpv	GT	Mloc	0.7	30.0
mdf	GT	Mloc	0.9	40.0
mhr	GT	Mloc	1.8	80.0
mrj	GT	Mloc	0.5	20.0
myv	GT	Mloc	1.2	50.0
sme	GT	Mloc	0.9	40.0
udm	GT	Mloc	0.5	20.0
avg.	GT	Mloc	1.1 ± 0.6	50 ± 30
med.	GT	Mloc	0.9 ± 0.3	40 ± 10
fin	MORF	ktok	898.0	100.0
kpv	MORF	ktok	11.0	1.2
mdf	MORF	ktok	64.0	7.1
mhr	MORF	ktok	15.0	1.7
mrj	MORF	ktok	353.0	39.3
myv	MORF	ktok	11.0	1.2
sme	MORF	ktok	9.0	1.1
udm	MORF	ktok	7.0	0.8
avg.	MORF	ktok	171 ± 296	19.1 ± 33.0
med.	MORF	ktok	13 ± 5	1.5 ± 0.5

Table 6: Transducer source complexity, in number of states per line of transducer source code. The column "LoC (M)" gives the number of lines of source code, in millions, and "States (k)" the size, in thousands of states of the compiled transducer.

Lang.	LoC (M)	States (k)	Complex.
fin	2.3	440.0	0.19
kpv	0.7	150.0	0.21
mdf	0.9	60.0	0.06
mhr	1.8	80.0	0.04
mrj	0.5	50.0	0.09
myv	1.2	110.0	0.09
sme	0.9	540.0	0.63
udm	0.5	60.0	0.14
avg.	1.1 ± 0.6	200 ± 200	0.2 ± 0.2
med.	0.9 ± 0.3	90 ± 40	0.12 ± 0.06

their performance is the same.

Figure 1 indicates that for the dictionary lookup task by-token, Morfessor with Wikipedia is more effort-efficient (relative to Finnish) for Komi-Zyrian, Udmurt, North Sámi, Erzya, Meadow Mari, and Giellatekno is more effort-efficient for Hill Mari. Remaining is Moksha, for which performance improvement scales with effort independent of model, and Finnish.

Since we normalise effort against Finnish, we can only observe that the Finnish Giellatekno model performs slightly better than the Finnish Wikipedia Morfessor model; efficiency claims cannot be made.

Figure 2 indicates that for the dictionary lookup task by-token, Morfessor with Wikipedia is more effort-efficient (relative to Finnish) for Komi-Zyrian only; Giellatekno remains more effort-efficient for Hill Mari. Meanwhile, Udmurt, North Sámi, Erzya, and Meadow Mari join Moksha in improvement scaling with effort; the spread in slopes (the rate at which performance improves as effort is increased) is, however, quite large.

Figure 3 shows that, as with lookup performance for tokens, Morfessor dominates vocabulary reduction efficiency, with only Hill Mari scaling with relative effort.

6 Conclusion

6.1 Discussion

There are many interesting things to notice in the effort-performance analysis.

Focusing just on the dictionary task, we find that compared against the same technology for Finnish, the Giellatekno North Sámi (`sme`) transducer has very high performance (relatively small ruleset), due to high rule complexity (the number of states is not very low). It is possible that North Sámi is simply easy to lemmatise, as Morfessor seems to do very well with a small corpus.

Hill Mari (`mrj`) shows predictable performance: relative to Finnish, a small increase in resources (going from 20% or 30% of Finnish resources for the Giellatekno transducer to 40% resources for the Wikipedia corpus) gives a modest increase in performance.

Overall, we see that percent improvement in tasks scales with effort (relative to Finnish) in the type-lookup task; in the token-lookup and vocabulary reduction tasks, performance improvement favours Morfessor. (That is, the Morfessor model has a higher improvement-to-resource ratio, with resources relative to Finnish.) This might be explained by the dramatic spread in Wikipedia corpus sizes used in the Morfessor models: median corpus size is 1.5% ± 0.5% the size of Finnish. Thus, improvement of 5% of the Morfessor model is increasing the nominal effort (kilotokens) by a factor of four, for the median corpus; compare with Giellatekno, where median model is 20% or 40% the size of the corresponding Finnish model, depending on the metric used. See the following section for potential avenues to control for this.

6.2 Future work

In the dictionary task, hits/words is lower than unique hits/words (see Section 5.1); this indicates that mislemmatised words are more frequent. Since irregular words are typically high-frequency, we might hypothesize that filtering these would close this gap. If not, it might point out areas for improvement in the lemmatisation algorithm.

We would like to also try other methods of lemmatising. One of the problems with the finite-state transducers is that they have limited capacity for lemmatising words which are not found in the lexicon. It is possible to use guesser techniques such as those described in Lindén (2009), but the accuracy is substantially lower than for hand-written entries. We would like to approach the problem as in Silfverberg and Tyers (2018) and train a sequence-to-sequence LSTM to perform lemmatisation using the finite-state transducer to produce forms for the training process.

There are other statistical methods, in particular byte-pair encoding and adaptor grammars (Johnson et al., 2006), which should be added to the comparison, and addition of further languages should be straightforward.

A more refined understanding of the relationship between size of corpus and Morfessor would give a richer dataset; this could be achieved by decimating the Wikipedia corpus. For truly low-resource languages, additional corpora may be necessary.

Similar refinement could be produced for the Giellatekno transducers using their version history: older versions of the transducers have had less work, and presumably have less source code. A dedicated researcher could compare various editions of the same transducer.

Cross-validation (in the case of Morfessor) and using multiple testing subcorpora would give some idea of the confidence of our performance measurements at the language-level.

Another interesting analysis, which we do not have the space to perform here, would be to normalise performance P, along the model axis m, for example for lan-

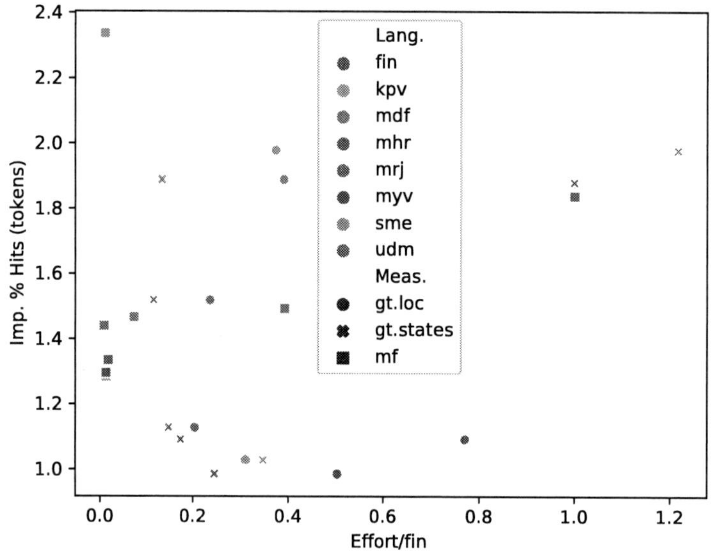

Figure 1: Improvement factor in hit rate in dictionary lookup (by tokens) (see Section 4.1; higher is better) vs. effort relative to Finnish (see Section 4.3; higher is more effort). In general, more effort-efficient models will appear to the upper-left of less effort-efficient models.

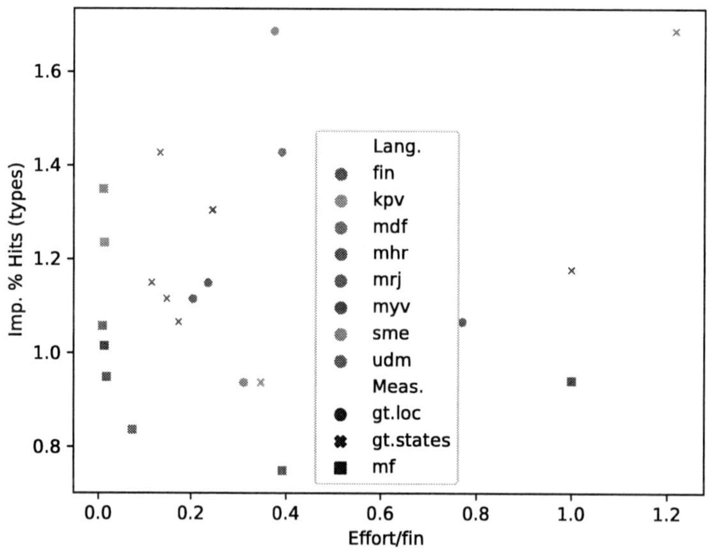

Figure 2: Improvement factor in hit rate in dictionary lookup (by types) (see Section 4.1; higher is better) vs. effort relative to Finnish (see Section 4.3; higher is more effort). In general, more effort-efficient models will appear to the upper-left of less effort-efficient models.

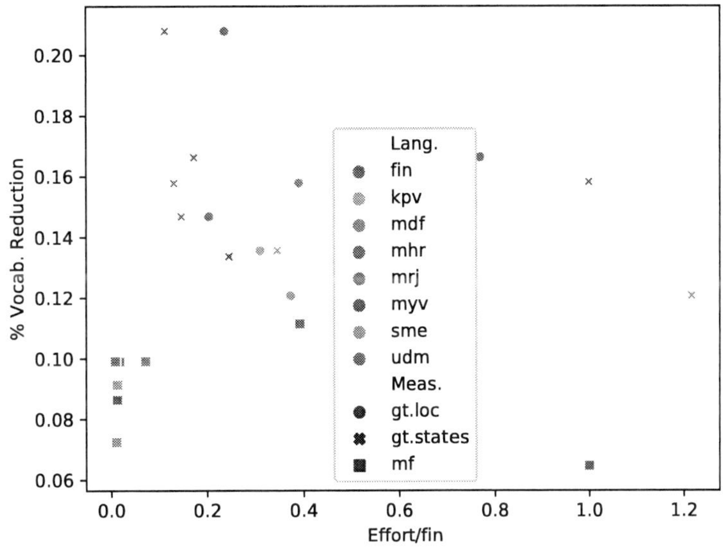

Figure 3: Vocabulary reduction performance in types (see Section 4.2; lower is better) vs. effort relative to Finnish (see Section 4.3; higher is more effort). In general, more effort-efficient models will appear to the lower-left of less effort-efficient models.

guage xxx (normalising against Giellatekno model performance):

$$P^*_{\mathtt{xxx},m} = P_{\mathtt{xxx},m} \cdot \frac{P_{\mathtt{fin},\mathrm{GT}}}{P_{\mathtt{fin},m}}$$

This measure, P^*, would always be fixed to 1.0 for Finnish, and would partially control for language-independent performance variation between models. This would then allow study of the distribution over languages of marginal performance improvement with effort.

References

Mark Johnson, Thomas L. Griffiths, and Sharon Goldwater. 2006. Adaptor grammars: A framework for specifying compositional nonparametric bayesian models. In *Advances in neural information processing systems*, pages 641–648.

Ryan Johnson, Lene Antonsen, and Trond Trosterud. 2013. Using finite state transducers for making efficient reading comprehension dictionaries. In *Proceedings of the 19th Nordic Conference of Computational Linguistics (NODALIDA 2013)*, 85, pages 59–71.

Krister Lindén. 2009. Guessers for finite-state transducer lexicons. *Computational Linguistics and Intelligent Text Processing 10th International Conference, CICLing 2009*, 5449:158–169.

Sjur Nørstebø Moshagen, Jack Rueter, Tommi Prinen, Trond Trosterud, and Francis Morton Tyers. 2014. Open-source infrastructures for collaborative work on under-resourced languages.

Miikka Silfverberg and Francis M. Tyers. 2018. Data-driven morphological analysis for Uralic languages. In *Proceedings of the 5th International Workshop on Computational Linguistics for the Uralic Languages (IWCLUL 2018)*.

Sami Virpioja, Peter Smit, Stig-Arne Grönroos, , and Mikko Kurimo. 2013. Morfessor 2.0: Python Implementation and Extensions for Morfessor Baseline. Technical report, Aalto University.

Eberhard Winkler. 2001. *Udmurt*. Lincom Europa.

On the questions in developing computational infrastructure for Komi-Permyak

Jack Rueter
University of Helsinki
jack.rueter@helsinki.fi

Niko Partanen
University of Helsinki
niko.partanen@helsinki.fi

Larisa Ponomareva
University of Helsinki
dojegpl@gmail.com

Abstract

There are two main written Komi varieties, Permyak and Zyrian. These are mutually intelligible but derive from different parts of the same Komi dialect continuum, representing the varieties prominent in the vicinity and in the cities of Syktyvkar and Kudymkar, respectively. Hence, they share a vast number of features, as well as the majority of their lexicon, yet the overlap in their dialects is very complex. This paper evaluates the degree of difference in these written varieties based on changes required for computational resources in the description of these languages when adapted from the Komi-Zyrian original. Primarily these changes include the FST architecture, but we are also looking at its application to the Universal Dependencies annotation scheme in the morphologies of the two languages.

Дженыта висьталӧм

Коми кылын кык гижан кыв: пермяцкӧй да зырянскӧй. Ӧтамӧд коласын нія вежӧртанаӧсь, но аркмисӧ нія разнӧй коми диалекттэзісь. Пермяцкӧй кыв олӧ Кудымкар лапӧлын, а зырянскӧй – Сыктывкар ладорын. Пермяцкӧй да зырянскӧй литературнӧй кыввезын эм уна ӧткодьыс, ӧткодьӧн лоӧ и ыджыт тор лексикаын, но ны диалектнӧй чертаэзлӧн пантасьӧмыс ӧддьӧн гардчӧм.

Эта статьяын мийӧ видзӧтам эна кык кывлісь ассямасӧ сы ладорсянь, мый ковсяс вежны лӧсьӧтӧм зырянскӧй вычислительнӧй ресурсісь, медбы керны сыись пермяцкӧйӧ. Медодз энӧ вежсьӧммесӧ колӧ керны FST-ын, но мийӧ сідзжӧ видзӧтам, кыдз FST лӧсялӧ Быдкодь Йитсьӧммезлӧн схемаӧ морфология ладорсянь.

1 Introduction

The Komi language is a member of the Permic branch of the Uralic language family. By nature, it is a pluricentric language, which, in addition to having two strong written traditions (Komi-Zyrian and Komi-Permyak), can be divided into several varieties. Although some of the other varieties do exhibit written use, no actual new written standards seem to be emerging (Цыпанов, 2009). Both Zyrian and Permyak have long and established written traditions, with continuous contemporary use. There are also numerous dialect resources currently available, i.e. Пономарева (2016) for Northern Permyak dialects.

Komi-Permyak and Komi-Zyrian are extremely agglutinative, but the two standards have different tendencies in their criteria for the definition of an orthographic word. Inflection mainly involves the use of suffixes, which, in the case of nominals, are NP final. Hence, contextual dropping of the head noun means that formatives shift to the next rightmost constituent of the NP.

While Komi-Zyrian has a long tradition of computerized morphological analysis, as finite-state transducers have been developed for it since the mid 1990s (Rueter, 2000), the computational resources for Komi-Permyak have been the focus of less intensive work. This article is intended as a roadmap for further development of Komi-Permyak computational resources. The morpho-

Proceedings of the 6th International Workshop on Computational Linguistics of Uralic Languages, pages 15–25
Wien, Austria, January 10 — 11, 2020.
https://doi.org/10.18653/v1/FIXME

logical features discussed in this paper have largely been already implemented in the FST in Giellatekno infrastructure, and the work has been primarily carried out by Jack Rueter. Ongoing work includes intense work on paradigmatic description by Larisa Ponomareva (Rueter et al., 2019a), which has been published within AKU-infrastructure. AKU is an abbreviation for *Avointa Kieliteknologiaa Uralilaisille/Uhanalaisille kielille* (Open language technology for Uralic/Endangered languages). Other projects that are directly associated with this are uralicNLP (Hämäläinen, 2019), Akusanat (Hämäläinen and Rueter, 2019b) and Ver'dd (Alnajjar et al., 2019) (see also *On Editing Dictionaries for Uralic Languages in an Online Environment*, in this publication). Forthcoming work includes the expansion of the initial Permyak treebank found in Universal Dependencies version 2.5 (Zeman et al., 2019), i.e. further work on what is scheduled for the next UD release, hence the underlying acuteness of further work with this often understudied, but central variety of Komi.

As the Komi-Zyrian finite state transducer has already reached a very advanced state, and the languages are so similar to one another, it is necessary to ask how far we can reuse the components of a Zyrian analyzer when working with Permyak. Although it has been suggested this kind of resource-sharing becomes most useful at higher levels of grammar, especially syntax Antonsen et al. (2010), in the case of very closely related languages the number of shared elements is considerable at all levels of the language. We understand this is a slippery road, and uttermost attention has to be paid to full respect of Permyak features and particularities, so that we do not simply force the Zyrian conventions upon Permyak. At the same time starting to develop a Permyak infrastructure from scratch feels like a missed opportunity to find some synchrony. In this article we attempt to describe all those particularities and pitfalls that have to be considered when one endeavors further the analysis of Permyak. Our approach is also in some sense comparable to that of (Pirinen, 2019).

As two Komi-Zyrian treebanks are also under continuous development (Partanen et al., 2018) it is particularly important to pay attention to Komi infrastructure at large. A recent survey of Uralic Universal Dependencies treebanks (Rueter and Partanen, 2019) showed that more work is needed to harmonize the annotation between languages, and working on closely related languages is certainly where similarity is most easily enforced but also most logically expected. In this context, it also has to be taken into account that several other smaller Uralic languages have had their own treebanks introduced in the past couple of years, e.g. Erzya (Rueter and Tyers, 2018), Karelian (Pirinen, 2019) and North Saami (Tyers and Sheyanova, 2017). This kind of work that concentrates more on manually annotated corpora complements the descriptive work on morphological analyzers extremely well. A well functioning morphological analyzer, however, seems to be one of the best starting points for further language technology, which provides a motivation for the work grounded in this paper.

Since this paper describes only the current, rather preliminary state of investigation, we have published the list of discussed features as an accompanying database (Rueter et al., 2020). This database is available online,[1] and can be extended as needed when a larger inventory of differing lexical items and syntactic constructions becomes available. Since we hope the comparative investigations reach other dialects and variants of the Permic languages, the database has been named accordingly with an optimistic mindset.

In this paper we have chosen to distinguish morphological suffixes from clitics with preceding hyphens. This will be achieved through the use of hyphens to set of morphological suffixes and equal signs to indicate clitics and other elements separated by a hyphen in the written norms. All examples in the paper, unless the source is given, have been created by Larisa Ponomareva.

2 Orthographic distinctions

During the development of the two Komi norms, a few orthographic distinctions have been made. These distinctions can be attributed to sub-dialect variation, on the one hand, and arbitrary spelling principles, on the other. The arbitrary spelling choices are simply orthographic, and do not necessarily relate to actual phonological differences in the languages.

Arbitrary choice involves the definition of word (i.e. written unit without white space) and the selection of background language form and letter combinations. It will be observed below that the Komi-Permyak converb paradigms are minimalis-

[1] `https://langdoc.github.io/comparative-permic-database`

tic in comparison to those of Komi-Zyrian. Komi-Permyak, on the one hand, tends to write separate words, and Komi-Zyrian tends to write single concatenated words, on the other. This can be exemplified in the converb paradigms for Komi-Permyak *-ик* /-ik/, which can only appear alone, in the singular illative or with possessive suffixes, whereas the Komi-Zyrian *-иг* /-ig/ converb also takes plural marking, cases, as well as numerous other elements *-öн* /-ən/, *-моз* /-moz/, *-тыр* /-tɨr/, *-тырйи* /-tɨrji/, *-тыръя* /-tɨrja/, *-кості* /-kosti/, *-коста* /-kosta/,... (Некрасова, 2000, p. 344–353)

Arbitrary character combinations can be illustrated best with two prominent paradigms: the geminate voiced palatal affricate is represented in Zyrian with *ддз ddz* but in Permyak this same affricate is rendered with *дзз dzz*. Consonants followed by a palatal glide and subsequent vowel are written using hard and soft sign combinations. In Zyrian, the norm is to use a soft sign following inherently soft consonants, whereas hard signs are used in other instances. In Permyak, on the contrary, the hard sign is used with specifically hard consonants, while the soft sign is used as default for other combinations.

One orthographic convention that works similarly in Permyak and Zyrian alike is *l : v* variation in stem-final position. This variation is not present in this form in any of the Komi-Permyak dialects, but as a literary convention it is shared with Zyrian standard. Permyak dialects, it will be noted, generally display a multitude of l-related subsystems (Баталова, 1982, p. 58).

Orthographic distinctions between the two Komi norms present few problems. On the one hand, computational distinctions are only attested in the use of the few paragogic consonants in alternate Permyak morphological forms. On the other, use of the NP plural in both variants appear to follow the same distribution, so any computational issue might only be found at the morpho-syntactic level.

3 Phonetical differences

The morpheme-final t / d correlation between Permyak and Zyrian is a prominent source of predictable morphological and lexical differences. This morpho-phonological difference is found word finally in the Permyak adjective *сьӧкыт* /ɕəkɨt/ and Zyrian *сьӧкыд* /ɕəkɨd/ 'heavy; difficult' as well as other corresponding pairs *-ыт* /-ɨt/ vs. *-ыд* /-ɨd/, Permyak and Zyrian respectively. It can also be observed in the causative derivation marker *-öт* /-ət/ vs. *-öд* /-əd/ in verb stems, such as *велöтны* /velətnɨ/ and *велöдны* /velədnɨ/ 'to teach', Permyak and Zyrian respectively. The same correlation is also found in the comitative case ending *-кöт* /-kət/ vs *-кöд* /kəd/ and the possessive suffixes for the second persons singular and plural: *-ыт* /-ɨt/ vs. *-ыд* /-ɨd/, and *-ныт* /-nɨt/ vs. *-ныд* /-nɨd/. The same voiceless vs voiced correlation might also be detected in the converbs *-икö* /-ikə/ vs *-игö* /-igə/, Permyak and Zyrian respectively.

On a similar note, there is a correlation between Permyak *ö* /-ə/ and Zyrian *-öй* /-əj/ in first person singular possessive marking. In verbal morphology, the Permyak morpheme-final *ö* /ə/ of the first person plural marker *-мö* /-mə/ corresponds to Zyrian endings *-м* /-m/, whereas the Zyrian first person plural imperative usage might include both *-мö* /-mə/ and *-мöй* /-məj/, as in *мунамöй* /munaməj/ 'let's go'.

4 Morphological differences

Many of the morphological forms provide an illustration of where the human learner may have problems in comprehension while the computer has no problems in computation. There are, however, numerous ways of how a minor difference in one morphological form has a potential impact on ambiguities in other parts of the system.

In this section we go through most essential differences in Komi-Zyrian and Komi-Permyak morphology.

4.1 Paragogical consonants

Both Komi language forms have the same paragogical consonants, but their distribution is varied. In practice, the so-called paragogic consonants are present when the stem is followed by a suffix with an onset vowel, and it is absent when word-final or followed by a consonant (cf. Безносикова et al., p. 16).

Paragogic consonants may be present in Permyak but to a lesser extent than they are in Zyrian due to sub-dialect representation, i.e. many of the sub-dialects do not have them. Komi-Zyrian includes paragogic consonants in its nominal declension and derivation – approximately 0.07 percent of the 12,046 noun stems in the Zyrian transducer have paragogic consonants, but this is reduced to 0.024 once the diminutive/material formative *тор* /tor/ is removed. Komi-Permyak, in contrast, limits its use of paragogic consonants in declensions, and the number of Komi-Permyak stems with paragogic

Permyak	*кыв*	+	*вез* (← -йэз)	*кыввез*
	/kɨv/	+	/vez (← -jez)/	/kɨvvez/
Zyrian	*кыв*	+	*яс*	*кывъяс*
	/kɨv/	+	/jas/	/kɨvjas/
	'word; language'	+	PL	'words; languages'

Figure 1: Example plural of /kɨv/ 'word; language'

Permyak	*му*	+	*эз*	*муэз*
	/mu/	+	/ez/	/muez/
Zyrian	*му*	+	*яс*	*муяс*
	/mu/	+	/jas/	/mujas/
	'land; country'	+	PL	'lands; countries'

Figure 2: Example plural of /mu/ 'land; country'

consonants is smaller. The Komi-Permyak standard language recognizes the paragogic consonants *й* /j/, *к* /k/ and *м* /m/ as alternative variants. The paragogic consonant *й* /j/ is more common than *к* /k/ and *м* /m/, the latter two are found only in a limited set of stems, such as *син* /ɕin/ : *синм-* /ɕinm-/ 'eye', *кос* /kos/ : *коск-* /kosk-/ 'lower back', *мыш* /mɨʃ/ : *мышк-* /mɨʃk/ 'back'. Thus the Komi-Permyak literary language supports the use of both *синмӧ пырӧ* /ɕinmə pyrə/ and *синӧ пырӧ* /ɕinə pyrə/ 'gets in the eye', where the analysis of *синмӧ* /ɕinmə/ and *синӧ* /ɕinə/ is eye.SG.ILL. (The paragogic *т* /t/ in the verb *локны* /loknɨ/ and *локт-* /lokt-/ 'to arrive' is the standard and cannot be left out of the paradigm in either of the literary languages.)

4.2 Plural formation

Phonological variation can be detected in the plural marking of NP heads, where the Zyrian normal plural marker involves the realization of *-яс* /-jas/, on the one hand, and the Permyak normal plural marker calls for either word-final consonant doubling (see fig 1) or, following a vowel, a simple *-эз* /-ez/ (see fig 2), on the other. Orthographically, the word-final consonant *й* /j/ forms an exception to this, here the Cyrillic *е* /je/ without orthographic duplication of *й* /j/ (see fig. 3).

Plural character duplication, which is the primary method of plural formation in Permyak, is also partially present in Zyrian dialects. This, however, is not accepted in the Zyrian written standard. Whereas Zyrian plural is formed with distinct suffix *-яс* /-jas/ (as illustrated in figures 1, 2, 3, above).

4.3 Possessive marking

Although singular possessive marking differs from Zyrian only through expected phonetic correspondence *t / d*, the plural forms display more complex assimilation. While the plural possessive forms in Zyrian are clearly segmentable, i.e. *понъяс* : *понъясыд* /ponjas/ : /pon-jas-ɨd/ dog-PL : dog-PL-2PSX, the corresponding forms for the second and third person in Permyak are often fused, i.e. *поннэз : поннэт* /pon-nez : pon-net/ dog-PL : dog-PL.2PSX (Лыткин, 1962). Forms with separate elements are, however, also possible. Both form types have already been implemented in the Permyak analyzer.

Permyak	*кай*	+	*ез*	*кайез*
	/kaj/	+	/jez/	/kajjez/
Zyrian	*кай*	+	*яс*	*кайяс*
	/kaj/	+	/jas/	/kajjas/
	'bird'	+	PL	'birds'

Figure 3: Example plural of /kaj/ 'bird'

4.4 Cases

While both literary norms generally describe the number of cases as being sixteen or seventeen, a reality check might be required. The most recent and extensive presentation of Komi-Zyrian, it should be noted, indicates at least 23 cases with new ones appearing all the time (Некрасова 2000:59–62). One reason for this inconsistency is the definition of case: What is a case, and what kinds of combinations they can be used in when speaking of a single referent and a double referent (inclusive elliptic referent). Thus we can observe organic expansion of the local cases and diversion in case enumerations.

Both language norms have regular extensions of the approximative case *-лань* /-laɲ/ 'towards X'. The case marker may take additional local case combinations, e.g. approximative + elative, in Permyak *-ланись* /-laɲ+iɕ/ and in Zyrian *-ланьысь* /-laɲ+iɕ/ 'from on towards X', which is actually just a more specific combination of semantics. Additional extensions mutual to both literary norms include the inessive, illative, prolative, terminative and egressive.

Diversity between Komi-Zyrian and Komi-Permyak is apparent in both phonetic variation and complementary distribution of morphology. This can be seen in regular nominal declension with regard to the prolative and terminative. The prolative *-ӧд* /-əd/ and translative *-ті* /-ti/, which are both regular declension in Komi-Zyrian, are only represented by a regular prolative *-ӧт* /-ət/ in Komi-Permyak. Albeit, an analogous transitive *-ті* /-ti/ is present present in Komi-Permyak in a few adpositions and adverbs, but it is not considered to be an independent case of its own.

Similarly, the two Komi-Permyak terminative cases in *-ӧдз* /-ədz/ and *-ви* /-vi/ are only represented by one terminative *-ӧдз* /-ədz/ in Komi-Zyrian. As a rule of thumb, we can say that the deviant Komi-Permyak *-ви* /-vi/ might be replaced in most places by *-ӧдз* /-ədz/, but research is still required to establish where the semantics of these two forms are distinct. Initially, it may be said that *-ви* /-vi/ can be used when indicating motion up to a boundary, whereas *-ӧдз* /-ədz/ implies both up to and passing that boundary.

Phonetic diversity is observed in the dative and elative cases. While the Zyrian dative is marked with *-лы* /-lɨ/, Permyak uses *-лӧ* /-lə/. Similarly, elative and ablative differ in their vowels. In Zyrian, the elative is marked with *-ысь* /-ɨɕ/ and the ablative with *-лысь* /-lɨɕ/, whereas in Permyak the corresponding forms are elative *-ись* /-iɕ/ and ablative *-лiсь* /-liɕ/

When inspecting NPS where the head has been deleted because it can be derived contextually, as discussed in the WALS chapter on adjectives without nouns (Gil, 2013), it will be noticed that Komi-Permyak uses a special accusative form for the accusative adjective without a head noun in *-ӧ* /-ə/, while the Komi-Zyrian solution in the same context is *-ӧс* /-əs/, see in Examples 1 and 2 below.

(1) тэныт гӧрдӧ али вежӧ сетны?

tenɨt	*gərd-ə*	*aʎi*	*veʒ-ə*	*ɕet-nɨ?*
2SG.DAT	red-ACC	or	yellow-ACC	give-INF

'shall [I] give you the red one or the yellow one?' (Permyak)

(2) Тэныд гӧрдӧс либӧ вежӧс сетны?

tenɨd	*gərd-əs*	*ʎibə*	*veʒ-əs*	*ɕet-nɨ?*
2SG.DAT	red-ACC	or	green-ACC	give-INF

'shall [I] give you the red one or the green one?' (Zyrian)

This difference, although seemingly small, has many implications for possible morphological analysis of such adjective forms. It creates ambiguity between adjective accusative, illative and possessive forms in a way that is not at all present in Zyrian. In addition, the resulting syntactic structure will need very distinct Constraint Grammar rules (Karlsson, 1990).

4.5 Case and possessive marker ordering

Possessive suffixes and case endings in the Komi-Permyak standard may appear in varied order, as illustrated in Example 3.

(3) каньыстӧг : каньтӧгъяс

kaɲɨstəg	*kaɲtəgjas*
cat-PxSG3-CAR	cat-CAR-PxSG3

'Without his / her cat' (Permyak)

Similar phenomena are also attested in Komi-Zyrian but not to the same extent (cf. Некрасова 2000, pp.54–95). Instead of changing the order of tags in the transducer according to morpheme order, an additional tag set for suffix ordering +So/CP *case, possession* and +So/PC *possession, case* has been adapted, as in the description of the two Mari standards (mhr) and (mrj) by Jeremy Bradley, Jack Rueter and Trond Trosterud at Giellatekno. The idea of the extra tag is to retain tag ordering used in testing and constraint grammar construction. In the meantime, an extra tag is made available for possible grammar research.

4.6 Verbal morphology

Both Permyak and Zyrian have dialect variation in verbal morphology, but in Permyak orthography more variation is accepted. For example, first and second person finite verb forms have a possibility to omit the final *-ӧ* /-ə/ in all tenses, both *мунам* /mun-am/ and *мунамӧ* /mun-amə/, for example, have identical meaning 'to_go-1PL.PRES'. Similar variation is also present in Zyrian dialects, but in the literary language it is not accepted, and the Zyrian FST returns an additional error tag.

In the second past tense third person singular, a different kind of variation is present in which *мунӧма* /munəma/ and and*мунӧм* /munəm/ with both being accepted. In Zyrian, only the first variant is in the literary standard. This has some impact to the possible tags of corresponding participles. In the second past tense second person singular, however, variation is present in the two possible forms such as *мунӧмат* /munəmat/ and *мунӧмыт* /munəmɨt/ 2SG.PST2. Again, there is no difference in meaning. The latter form is directly comparable to the Zyrian form *мунӧмыд* /munəmɨd/ through a phonological difference already described above, see Section 3.

In the third person plural present the variation is similar, but with different elements: *мунӧны* /munənɨ/ and *мунӧн* /munən/ 'to_go-3PL.PRES'.

Again, there is no conceivable difference in meaning. The shorter form seems to be used more in the spoken language. This variation is not present in any form in Zyrian.

There are parts of Permyak verbal morphology that have no counterparts in the Zyrian standard language. One of the most frequent differing forms are the third person plural past and future indicative verb forms. In Permyak, the paradigm in past, present and future can be illustrated with the verb *мунны* /munnɨ/ 'to go', *мунісӧ* : *мунӧны* (or *мунӧн*) : *мунасӧ* /munisə/ : /munənɨ/ (or /munən/) : /munasə/. In Zyrian the corresponding paradigm would be *мунісны* : *мунӧны мунасны* /munisnɨ/ : /munənɨ/ : /munasnɨ/, which illustrates how forms with *-sə* are lacking.

Permyak past tense formation is more regular than Zyrian, which displays complex variation in possible homonymy for first and third person past tense forms of some intransitive verbs, such that *муні* /muni/ could be both a first or third person singular form. In Permyak, the only verb that displays this variation is *вӧвны* /vəvnɨ/ 'to be', whereas other verbs are regularly marked: *муні* /mun-i/ to_go-1SG.PST *муніс* /mun-is/ to_go-3SG.PST.

In the Permyak second past tense the form *мунӧмась* /munəmaɕ/ corresponds to Zyrian *мунӧмаӧсь* /munəmaəɕ/. Here the morpheme suffixation in Zyrian is more transparent. Similar forms are also possible in Zyrian dialects, but they do not occur in the written standard. From the perspective of morphological analyzer construction, these forms pose no challenge.

Permyak connegatives are formed differently from their Zyrian counterparts, so that Permyak plural connegative is always marked with *-ӧ* /-ə/, e.g. *оз мунӧ* 'he/she does not go' : *озӧ мунӧ* 'they do not go' /oz munə/ : /ozə munə/. In Zyrian, the plural connegative would be formed as *оз мунны* /oz munnɨ/ 'they do not go', with the connegative form identical to the infinitive of the verb. In this detail, the Permyak connegative is less ambiguous than Zyrian, and i.e. some of the Constraint Grammar rules that disambiguate this currently in Zyrian would not be needed.

Another difference associated with connegatives is the second person plural negation verb forms *од* /od/ and *одӧ* /odə/ in Permyak, which are distinct from their Zyrian counterparts *он* /on/ and *онӧ* /onə/. The same stem is also present in past tense forms, and regularly matches the past tense paradigm with stem initial *э-* /e-/. The variation in vowel in the end behaves as already described above.

Permyak imperatives have multiple forms not found in Zyrian. Forms created with *-те* /-ce/, e.g. *мунӧте* /munəce/ 'go-IMP.2PL' and *босьтӧте* /boɕtəce/ 'take-IMP.2PL', do not differ in their meaning from more common imperative forms, such as *мунӧ* /munə/ 'go-IMP.2PL' and *босьтӧ* /boɕtə/ 'take-IMP.2PL'. The former forms, however, may be more colloquial (Лыткин, 1962, 249). Forms marked with *-те -се* are present in plural first and second persons.

Another type of imperative is formed with *-ко* /-ko/. In the orthography it is written with a hyphen. It is used in second person singular, and in the first and second person plural. This imperative has a softer meaning, more of a request than a command. We use the tag +Prec, as in precative[2]. This form is a direct parallel to the Russian *-ка* /-ka/, which also indicates a request, e.g. *возьмите-ка* /voʑmice-ka/ 'do take [it]'.

Related to imperatives, the optative is formed in Permyak written language with two particles *ась* /aɕ/ and *мед* /med/. The former particle does not exist in Komi-Zyrian.

The converb system in Permyak displays some characteristics not found in Zyrian. One difference is uniquely the Permyak converb *-тӧн* /-tən/. It expresses simultaneous action of two verbs.

(4) муні сывтӧн

mun-i *ɕɨv-tən*
go-1SG.PST sing-CNV

'I went singing' (Permyak)

Besides converb forms that are not marked for person, there are also forms with possessive suffixes. These, unexpectedly, occur with palatalization and gemination of the stem-final consonant, as in:

(5) муні сывтӧнням

mun-i *ɕɨv-təɲːam*
go-1SG.PST sing-CNV.1SG

'I went singing' (Permyak)

In fact, this palatalization and concurrent gemination occurs in other possessive forms, too:

[2] https://glossary.sil.org/term/precative-mood

(6) увтӧттяс

uvt-əcːas
under-PRL.PxSg3

'(to go) under (something)' (Permyak)

In this latter form the prolative and possessive suffix are not clearly separable, which again illustrates the more fusional morphology of Permyak when compared to Zyrian. (Looking back at the plural morpheme, it will be noted that palatalization is a distinguishing factor in the possessive forms)

Another converb that lacks a complete correspondence in Komi is the Permyak *-ик* /-ik/. In Zyrian there is a cognate converb *-иг* /-ig/, and this form also expresses simultaneous action as the Permyak *-тӧн* /-tən/ converb discussed above. There are, however, small differences between the languages. In Permyak the converb when not used as an unmarked complement is always used with the unambiguous illative case or the ambiguous illative case with possessive suffixing, whereas in Zyrian the instrumental is used in the forms that are not marked for possessor. In both languages, however, the possessive forms are deductively in the illative (as determined by the semantic use of the illative), and they are structurally formed in identical way, i.e. *мун-ікас* /mun-ikas/ go-CNV.ILL.3SG, Zyrian *мун-ігас* /mun-igas/ go-CNV.ILL.3SG 'while going'

4.7 Derivational morphology

There are individual derivational morphemes that are present in Permyak but not in Zyrian. There is *-жуг* /-ʒug/ that forms pejoratives, and multiple diminutives such as *-ок* /-ok/, *-очка* /-ot͡ɕka/ and *-иньӧй* /-iɲəj/.

In adjective formation, Permyak has several particular features. It is possible to form new adjectives from nouns with suffix *-овӧй* /-ovəj/ (Лыткин, 1962, p. 14) Additionally, *-ӧв* /-əv/ forms excessive adjectives and adverbs, i.e. *ыджыт* : *ыджытӧв* /ɨdʒːit/ : /ɨdʒːitəv/ 'large : too large'.

There are also numerous derivation types that are found in Zyrian, but are not present in Permyak (Лыткин, 1962, p. 14) *-лун* /-lun/, *-шой* /ʃoj/ and *-ук* /-uk/. As corresponding forms do not exist, the analyzer should either provide no analysis for them, or possibly mark them with a tag indicating they are non-standard.

5 Clitics

Discourse clitic marking in Komi-Zyrian is a salient source of morphological ambiguity. While both *=сӧ* /=sə/ and *=мӧ* /=tə/ can be interpreted as clitics, they also represent the accusative case with third person singular and second person singular possessive marking, respectively. As these clitics do not occur in Permyak, such a homonymy is not present in the paradigm, making disambiguation of Permyak less problematic.

There are two discourse clitics commonly used in Permyak, *=ту* /=tu/ and *=то* /=to/. Both occur in the written standard, with their origin possibly in varied dialect distributions. In Zyrian dialects, a corresponding clitic in *=то* /=to/ is also present, but the most important factor here is that, as explained above, while these clitics take the role of Zyrian *=сӧ* /=sə/ and *=мӧ*, they also make Permyak accusatives much less ambigious than those in Zyrian.

With the infinitive forms of Permyak verbs, a form identical to Zyrian *=мӧ* /=tə/ does occur (Баталова, 1975, p. 188), but the amount of ambiguity this introduces is not as problematic as what is seen in Zyrian.

Question marking in the two Komis presents a dichotomy of *=ӧ* /=ə/ in Komi-Zyrian and an independent particle *я* /ja/ in Komi-Permyak. Anticipation of a shallow-transfer translation system, raises the question of how these equivalent items might be designated for both languages regardless of orthographic conventions. (In Western tradition, the question is one of the four traditional sentence types, so there should be a way to address it in the code.)

6 Universal Dependencies

Work with the 2.5 release of the Komi-Permyak Universal Dependencies treebank (UD_Komi_Permyak-UH) has emphasized the need for consistency with the existing Zyrian treebanks. Since the Zyrian treebanks are relatively small, it is still easy to propose changes for both treebank sets, and future work with Zyrian also needs to be considered in the Permyak treebank.

As Permyak and Zyrian are very closely related languages, the development of different treebanks will certainly be mutually beneficial. There has been recent interest to use resources from related or contact languages in order to train tools such as dependency parsers (i.e. Lim et al., 2018), but, in the case of Komi-Zyrian, none of the languages in the Universal Dependencies project have been particularly close to Komi, and the results have not been at so high a level that such models could have been applied in language documentation work. With Komi-Permyak and Komi-Zyrian, multilingual model training of this type may very well be worth the effort, as the grammatical structures and lexicon are largely shared. The benefits become particularly clear when attempts are made to process dialect materials in either language, as the distribution of features is in many ways different from those of the written standards (further discussion of which, unfortunately, is outside the scope of this paper).

The Komi-Permyak treebank, once again, underscores the need for a different approach to representative sentence selection. While large treebank projects are able to utilize large amounts of data with inherited but transferable annotation from other projects, small languages, such as Komi-Permyak and Komi-Zyrian, cannot really opt for statistical representation. Instead, it is proposed that features specific to the language be selected. Hence, part of the strategy for the initial release of the Komi-Permyak treebank was to feature numerals and their regular morpho-semantic use, e.g. both Komi standards have multiplicative-distributional numerals as well as ordinal-multiplicative numerals. Komi-Permyak, however, has an additional *a*-final numeral used in copula complement position to indicate the notion of a tallied sum, e.g.

(7) Деревняын оліссес нёля.

ɟerevɲa-ɨn	*oliɕ:es*	*ɲoʎ-a*
village-INE	dweller.PL	four-A

'In the village, there are four people all together' (Permyak)

One approach could be to select example sentences from available Komi grammars, as this way it would be possible to make different grammatical phenomena fully represented. There are many features of Komi that are typologically relevant, but relatively rare, as already discussed in Partanen et al. (2018). These include, among other features, various stacked cases that occur only sporadically in all their realizations even in a very large written corpora.

7 Possibilities for resource reuse

While the morphological analyzer is still being developed for Permyak, with the groundwork for it largely copied from the existing Zyrian analyzer, special attention must be paid to the particularities of Permyak and the reduction of interference from the original Zyrian. One approach that needs further work is to ensure that both Permyak and Zyrian YAML tests are comparable in their coverage, which would also allow further automatic testing of how large the number of shared forms is. This, for example, would require the writing of YAML tests for Komi-Zyrian, which has few tests on the whole.

Permyak and Zyrian also share a extensive majority of their lexicon. This leaves the question open as to how exactly we should proceed with the management of the lexicographic data for these languages, i.e. while using tools such as Akusanat and Verdd (see i.e. Rueter and Hämäläinen, 2017; Hämäläinen and Rueter, 2019b). One also has to ask whether there are specific ways on how Permyak and Zyrian lexical resources should be connected to each other. This might be solved with cognate searching analogical to what has been used for Northern Sami and Skolt Sami cognates for establishing initial etymological associations (Hämäläinen and Rueter, 2019a). Russian loanwords, although differently adapted are largely shared. At present, this issue has been partially solved through the sharing of proper nouns mutual to nearly all languages written in Russian Cyrillics[3] (49,156 words) and additional adjectives shared by both Komi transducers [4] (~6000 words), whose content was initially introduced in FU-Lab for adjectives ending in *-öй* /-əj/. The shared kom-adjectives-russian-like.lexc file has preliminarily been selected on the pretext that the Komi letter *ö* cannot occur twice in a given Komi-Permyak stem. Further editing of this file will be required to remove Komi-Zyrian instances of *-öй* /-əj/ where the Russian equivalent would indicate a stressed vowel. When the Russian equivalent has a stressed *-o*, the Permyak variant is also *-o*.

It must be mentioned that through our meticulous work on Komi-Permyak analyzer, we have arrived at a situation where there are more YAML tests for Permyak than for Zyrian. It could be an interesting idea to make sure that Permyak and Zyr-

[3]gtsvn/giella-shared/urj-Cyrl/src/morphology/stems/urj-Cyrl-propernouns.lexc

[4]gtsvn/langs/kpv/src/morphology/stems/kom-adjectives-russian-like.lexc

ian tests contain the same lexemes with their matching analyses. The forms would be different, but this would allow comparing the paradigms from one more perspective. (In fact, this can be rendered rather easily by generating a separate full Zyrian YAML test for every lexeme addressed in the Permyak YAML tests, but it will also require native-like language knowledge for proof-reading. (Rueter et al., 2019b)) In addition, at least the forms that categorically do not exist in the Permyak should not be getting a reading, but the situation becomes more complicated with the forms shared by various Zyrian and Permyak dialects. (Here, we will need to use the descriptive YAML tests. As there are already three categories of YAML tests in the Giella infrastructure: dict[ionary], norm[ative] and desc[riptive]) Probably, some additional distinctions will be made between the descriptive and normative analyzers, with the first being less restricted, as has been done with Zyrian earlier. (Analogical work has been done in this vein with development of the Võro language YAML tests due to the extensively descriptive nature originally depicted in the transducer to cover various dialects (Iva and Rueter, 2020))

8 Conclusion

Based to our analysis, developing a Komi-Permyak FST based on the Komi-Zyrian FST is a worthwhile and relatively straightforward process. We also believe that there are ways to use such analyzers for better identification and quantification of the differences between these pluricentric varieties.

The approach taken in this paper, with a detailed description of the morphological differences encountered between the two norms, is believed to render a more legible work flow. Such a plan helps to formulate strategies for development and further work on the Komi-Permyak analyzer and treebanks.

One of the upcoming tasks is to extend this work from the literary languages into various dialects, as has already been done with the Zyrian analyzer. This will further complicate the relationship between work done on Permyak and Zyrian, as the feature isoglosses usually have distributions that do not follow the official language boundaries. Although smaller Komi varieties such as Zyuzdin and Yazva have some resources and recent publishing activities (for Yazva i.e. Паршакова, 2003), it is currently unclear in which forms the existing resources on these languages should be integrated into the infrastructure described here.

Our analysis is based on standard grammatical references to Komi-Permyak, so if there are features that need to be addressed further, they might be something that earlier literature has either neglected or failed to notice. Thus the development of a computational infrastructure becomes better anchored in the grammatical description of Komi-Permyak, and the relationship of these often remote, although closely connected activities, becomes more firmly established.

Acknowledgments

Jack Rueter has been able to participate in these developments while performing expertise work on Uralic languages for a FINCLARIN project at the University of Helsinki, Digital Humanities Department. Special thanks to the University of Helsinki for funding Rueter's travel.

Niko Partanen works within the project Language Documentation meets Language Technology: The Next Step in the Description of Komi, funded by the Kone Foundation, Finland. Special thanks to the University of Helsinki for funding Partanen's travel.

Larisa Ponomareva is presently working as a research assistant at the University of Helsinki, Digital Humanities with funding from the Finnish Social Insurance Institution (KELA).

References

K. Alnajjar, M. Hämäläinen, N. Partanen, and Jack Rueter. 2019. The open dictionary infrastructure for uralic languages. In *Электронная письменность народов Российской Федерации: Опыт, проблемы и перспективы. Материалы II Международной научной конференции (Уфа, 11–12 декабря 2019 г.)*, pages 49–51.

Lene Antonsen, Trond Trosterud, and Linda Wiechetek. 2010. Reusing grammatical resources for new languages. In *Proceedings of the Seventh International Conference on Language Resources and Evaluation (LREC'10)*, Valletta, Malta. European Language Resources Association (ELRA).

David Gil. 2013. Adjectives without nouns. In Matthew S. Dryer and Martin Haspelmath, editors, *The World Atlas of Language Structures Online*. Max Planck Institute for Evolutionary Anthropology, Leipzig.

Mika Hämäläinen. 2019. UralicNLP: An NLP library for Uralic languages. *Journal of Open Source Software*, 4(37):1345.

Mika Hämäläinen and Jack Rueter. 2019a. Finding Sami cognates with a Character-Based NMT Approach. In *Proceedings of the Workshop on Computational Methods for Endangered Languages*, volume 1.

Mika Hämäläinen and Jack Rueter. 2019b. An open online dictionary for endangered uralic languages. *Electronic lexicography in the 21st century (eLex 2019): Smart lexicography.*

Sulev Iva and Jack Rueter. 2020. rueter/aku-morph-voro: Basic adjectives, nouns and verbs.

Fred Karlsson. 1990. Constraint grammar as a framework for parsing running text. In *COLNG 1990 Volume 3: Papers presented to the 13th International Conference on Computational Linguistics.*

KyungTae Lim, Niko Partanen, and Thierry Poibeau. 2018. Multilingual dependency parsing for low-resource languages: Case studies on North Saami and Komi-Zyrian.

Niko Partanen, Rogier Blokland, KyungTae Lim, Thierry Poibeau, and Michael Rießler. 2018. The first Komi-Zyrian Universal Dependencies treebanks. In *Second Workshop on Universal Dependencies (UDW 2018), November 2018, Brussels, Belgium*, pages 126–132.

Tommi A Pirinen. 2019. Building minority dependency treebanks, dictionaries and computational grammars at the same time—an experiment in Karelian treebanking. In *Proceedings of the Third Workshop on Universal Dependencies (UDW, SyntaxFest 2019)*, pages 132–136.

Jack Rueter and Mika Hämäläinen. 2017. Synchronized Mediawiki based analyzer dictionary development. In *International Workshop for Computational Linguistics of Uralic Languages*, pages 1–7. Association for Computational Linguistics.

Jack Rueter and Niko Partanen. 2019. Survey of Uralic Universal Dependencies development. In *Workshop on Universal Dependencies*, page 78. Association for Computational Linguistics.

Jack Rueter, Niko Partanen, and Larisa Ponomareva. 2019a. rueter/aku-morph-komi-permyak: Basic nouns, verbs and pronouns.

Jack Rueter, Niko Partanen, and Larisa Ponomareva. 2019b. rueter/aku-morph-komi-zyrian: Basic nouns, verbs and pronouns.

Jack Rueter, Niko Partanen, and Larisa Ponomareva. 2020. langdoc/comparative-permic-database: Comparative Permic Database.

Jack Rueter and Francis Tyers. 2018. Towards an open-source universal-dependency treebank for Erzya. In *Proceedings of the 4th International Workshop on Computational Linguistics for Uralic languages*, pages 106–118. ACL.

Jack M. Rueter. 2000. Хельсинкиса университетын кыв туялысь Ижкарын перымса симпозиум вылын лыддьӧмтор. In *Пермистика 6 (Proceedings of Permistika 6 conference)*, pages 154–158.

Francis M Tyers and Mariya Sheyanova. 2017. Annotation schemes in North Sámi dependency parsing. In *Proceedings of the Third Workshop on Computational Linguistics for Uralic Languages*, pages 66–75.

Daniel Zeman, Joakim Nivre, Mitchell Abrams, Noëmi Aepli, Željko Agić, Lars Ahrenberg, Gabrielė Aleksandravičiūtė, Lene Antonsen, Katya Aplonova, Maria Jesus Aranzabe, Gashaw Arutie, Masayuki Asahara, Luma Ateyah, Mohammed Attia, Aitziber Atutxa, Liesbeth Augustinus, Elena Badmaeva, Miguel Ballesteros, Esha Banerjee, Sebastian Bank, Verginica Barbu Mititelu, Victoria Basmov, Colin Batchelor, John Bauer, Sandra Bellato, Kepa Bengoetxea, Yevgeni Berzak, Irshad Ahmad Bhat, Riyaz Ahmad Bhat, Erica Biagetti, Eckhard Bick, Agnė Bielinskienė, Rogier Blokland, Victoria Bobicev, Loïc Boizou, Emanuel Borges Völker, Carl Börstell, Cristina Bosco, Gosse Bouma, Sam Bowman, Adriane Boyd, Kristina Brokaitė, Aljoscha Burchardt, Marie Candito, Bernard Caron, Gauthier Caron, Tatiana Cavalcanti, Gülşen Cebiroğlu Eryiğit, Flavio Massimiliano Cecchini, Giuseppe G. A. Celano, Slavomír Čéplö, Savas Cetin, Fabricio Chalub, Jinho Choi, Yongseok Cho, Jayeol Chun, Alessandra T. Cignarella, Silvie Cinková, Aurélie Collomb, Çağrı Çöltekin, Miriam Connor, Marine Courtin, Elizabeth Davidson, Marie-Catherine de Marneffe, Valeria de Paiva, Elvis de Souza, Arantza Diaz de Ilarraza, Carly Dickerson, Bamba Dione, Peter Dirix, Kaja Dobrovoljc, Timothy Dozat, Kira Droganova, Puneet Dwivedi, Hanne Eckhoff, Marhaba Eli, Ali Elkahky, Binyam Ephrem, Olga Erina, Tomaž Erjavec, Aline Etienne, Wograine Evelyn, Richárd Farkas, Hector Fernandez Alcalde, Jennifer Foster, Cláudia Freitas, Kazunori Fujita, Katarína Gajdošová, Daniel Galbraith, Marcos Garcia, Moa Gärdenfors, Sebastian Garza, Kim Gerdes, Filip Ginter, Iakes Goenaga, Koldo Gojenola, Memduh Gökırmak, Yoav Goldberg, Xavier Gómez Guinovart, Berta González Saavedra, Bernadeta Griciūtė, Matias Grioni, Normunds Grūzītis, Bruno Guillaume, Céline Guillot-Barbance, Nizar Habash, Jan Hajič, Jan Hajič jr., Mika Hämäläinen, Linh Hà Mỹ, Na-Rae Han, Kim Harris, Dag Haug, Johannes Heinecke, Felix Hennig, Barbora Hladká, Jaroslava Hlaváčová, Florinel Hociung, Petter Hohle, Jena Hwang, Takumi Ikeda, Radu Ion, Elena Irimia, Ọlájídé Ishola, Tomáš Jelínek, Anders Johannsen, Fredrik Jørgensen, Markus Juutinen, Hüner Kaşıkara, Andre Kaasen, Nadezhda Kabaeva, Sylvain Kahane, Hiroshi Kanayama, Jenna Kanerva, Boris Katz, Tolga Kayadelen, Jessica Kenney, Václava Kettnerová, Jesse Kirchner, Elena Klementieva, Arne Köhn, Kamil Kopacewicz, Natalia Kotsyba, Jolanta Kovalevskaitė, Simon Krek, Sookyoung Kwak, Veronika Laippala, Lorenzo Lambertino, Lucia Lam, Tatiana Lando, Septina Dian Larasati, Alexei Lavrentiev, John Lee, Phương Lê Hồng,

Alessandro Lenci, Saran Lertpradit, Herman Leung, Cheuk Ying Li, Josie Li, Keying Li, KyungTae Lim, Maria Liovina, Yuan Li, Nikola Ljubešić, Olga Loginova, Olga Lyashevskaya, Teresa Lynn, Vivien Macketanz, Aibek Makazhanov, Michael Mandl, Christopher Manning, Ruli Manurung, Cătălina Mărănduc, David Mareček, Katrin Marheinecke, Héctor Martínez Alonso, André Martins, Jan Mašek, Yuji Matsumoto, Ryan McDonald, Sarah McGuinness, Gustavo Mendonça, Niko Miekka, Margarita Misirpashayeva, Anna Missilä, Cătălin Mititelu, Maria Mitrofan, Yusuke Miyao, Simonetta Montemagni, Amir More, Laura Moreno Romero, Keiko Sophie Mori, Tomohiko Morioka, Shinsuke Mori, Shigeki Moro, Bjartur Mortensen, Bohdan Moskalevskyi, Kadri Muischnek, Robert Munro, Yugo Murawaki, Kaili Müürisep, Pinkey Nainwani, Juan Ignacio Navarro Horñiacek, Anna Nedoluzhko, Gunta Nešpore-Bērzkalne, Lương Nguyễn Thị, Huyền Nguyễn Thị Minh, Yoshihiro Nikaido, Vitaly Nikolaev, Rattima Nitisaroj, Hanna Nurmi, Stina Ojala, Atul Kr. Ojha, Adédayọ̀ Olúòkun, Mai Omura, Petya Osenova, Robert Östling, Lilja Øvrelid, Niko Partanen, Elena Pascual, Marco Passarotti, Agnieszka Patejuk, Guilherme Paulino-Passos, Angelika Peljak-Łapińska, Siyao Peng, Cenel-Augusto Perez, Guy Perrier, Daria Petrova, Slav Petrov, Jason Phelan, Jussi Piitulainen, Tommi A Pirinen, Emily Pitler, Barbara Plank, Thierry Poibeau, Larisa Ponomareva, Martin Popel, Lauma Pretkalniņa, Sophie Prévost, Prokopis Prokopidis, Adam Przepiórkowski, Tiina Puolakainen, Sampo Pyysalo, Peng Qi, Andriela Rääbis, Alexandre Rademaker, Loganathan Ramasamy, Taraka Rama, Carlos Ramisch, Vinit Ravishankar, Livy Real, Siva Reddy, Georg Rehm, Ivan Riabov, Michael Rießler, Erika Rimkutė, Larissa Rinaldi, Laura Rituma, Luisa Rocha, Mykhailo Romanenko, Rudolf Rosa, Davide Rovati, Valentin Roşca, Olga Rudina, Jack Rueter, Shoval Sadde, Benoît Sagot, Shadi Saleh, Alessio Salomoni, Tanja Samardžić, Stephanie Samson, Manuela Sanguinetti, Dage Särg, Baiba Saulīte, Yanin Sawanakunanon, Nathan Schneider, Sebastian Schuster, Djamé Seddah, Wolfgang Seeker, Mojgan Seraji, Mo Shen, Atsuko Shimada, Hiroyuki Shirasu, Muh Shohibussirri, Dmitry Sichinava, Aline Silveira, Natalia Silveira, Maria Simi, Radu Simionescu, Katalin Simkó, Mária Šimková, Kiril Simov, Aaron Smith, Isabela Soares-Bastos, Carolyn Spadine, Antonio Stella, Milan Straka, Jana Strnadová, Alane Suhr, Umut Sulubacak, Shingo Suzuki, Zsolt Szántó, Dima Taji, Yuta Takahashi, Fabio Tamburini, Takaaki Tanaka, Isabelle Tellier, Guillaume Thomas, Liisi Torga, Trond Trosterud, Anna Trukhina, Reut Tsarfaty, Francis Tyers, Sumire Uematsu, Zdeňka Urešová, Larraitz Uria, Hans Uszkoreit, Andrius Utka, Sowmya Vajjala, Daniel van Niekerk, Gertjan van Noord, Viktor Varga, Eric Villemonte de la Clergerie, Veronika Vincze, Lars Wallin, Abigail Walsh, Jing Xian Wang, Jonathan North Washington, Maximilan Wendt, Seyi Williams, Mats Wirén, Christian Wittern, Tsegay Woldemariam, Tak-sum Wong, Alina Wróblewska, Mary Yako, Naoki Yamazaki, Chunxiao Yan, Koichi Yasuoka, Marat M. Yavrumyan, Zhuoran Yu, Zdeněk Žabokrtský, Amir Zeldes, Manying Zhang, and Hanzhi Zhu. 2019. Universal dependencies 2.5. LINDAT/CLARIN digital library at the Institute of Formal and Applied Linguistics (ÚFAL), Faculty of Mathematics and Physics, Charles University.

Р. М. Баталова. 1975. *Коми-пермяцкая диалектология*. М.: Наука.

Р. М. Баталова. 1982. *Ареальные исследования по восточным финно-угорским языкам: Коми языки*. М.: Наука.

Л. М. Безносикова, Е. А. Айбабина, and Р. И. Коснырева. *Коми-роч кывчукӧр, publisher = Сыктывкар: Коми небӧг лэдзанiн, year=2000*.

В. И. Лыткин. 1962. *Коми-пермяцкий язык: учебник для высших учебных заведений*. Кудымкар: Коми пермяцкое книжное издательство.

Г. Некрасова. 2000. Эмакыв. In Г. В. Федюнёва, editor, *Öнiя коми кыв, морфология*. Россияса наукаяс академия, Коми наука шӧрин, Сыктывкар.

А. Л. Паршакова. 2003. *Коми-язьвинский букварь. Учебное издание*. Пермь: Пермское книжное издательство.

Л. Г. Пономарева. 2016. *Ойвывся коми-пермяккезлӧн сёрни*. М.: Быдкодь Отирлӧн кыввез.

Йӧлгинь Цыпанов. 2009. Перым кывъяслӧн талунъя серпас. *Suomalais-Ugrilaisen Seuran Toimituksia = Mémoires de la Société Finno-Ougrienne*, 258:191–206.

On Editing Dictionaries for Uralic Languages in an Online Environment

Khalid Alnajjar
Department of
Computer Science
University of Helsinki
khalid.alnajjar
@helsinki.fi

Mika Hämäläinen
Department of
Digital Humanities
University of Helsinki
mika.hamalainen
@helsinki.fi

Jack Rueter
Department of
Digital Humanities
University of Helsinki
jack.rueter
@helsinki.fi

Abstract

We present an open online infrastructure for editing and visualization of dictionaries of different Uralic languages (e.g. Erzya, Moksha, Skolt Sami and Komi-Zyrian). Our infrastructure integrates fully into the existing Giellatekno one in terms of XML dictionaries and FST morphology. Our code is open source, and the system is being actively used in editing a Skolt Sami dictionary set to be published in 2020.

Abstract

Tämä artikkeli esittelee Uralilaisten kielten (kuten ersän, mokshan, koltansaamen ja komi-syrjäänin) sanakirjojen toimittamiseen ja visualisointiin tarkoitetun avoimen verkkoinfrastruktuurin. Meidän infrastruktuurimme integroituu Giellateknoon XML-sanakirjojen ja FST-morfologian osalta. Lähdekoodimme on avointa, ja järjestelmäämme käytetään tällä hetkellä aktiivisesti koltansaamen sanakirjan toimitustyössä. Koltan sanakirja julkaistaan vuonna 2020.

1 Introduction

In order to revitalize severely endangered languages, such as many of the Uralic languages, enormous work is required to collect as many resources and knowledge about them as possible, while also involving their native communities. Digitizing the resources of endangered languages is crucial as it boosts the language resources in various ways, such as preserving them in a versioned manner and facilitating access to them globally. Scholars have produced valuable lexicographic resources (such as dictionaries and finite-state transducers) for endangered Uralic languages (e.g. Komi-Zyrian, Ingrian, Erzya, Moksha and Skolt Sami) in order to revitalize them.

We present a large-scale open-source MediaWiki-based dictionary for such languages, (named Akusanat) (c.f. Hämäläinen and Rueter 2018) and a customly-built and user-friendly web system (named Ve′rdd[1]) that improves and amending the knowledge presented in such dictionaries. As MediaWiki sets some limitations to the structure of the system both on the back-end in terms of the database and on the front-end in terms of usability, the external, yet integrated system, Ver′dd is set to tackle these limitations.

It is also worth noting that one use case where such dictionary interfaces could be very useful is language documentation. Although the field has been slow to adopt language technology, there have been significant recent advancements in integrating it into projects workflows (Blokland et al., 2015; Блокланд et al., 2014). One aspect where this has not yet been done is lexicography, which, however, is usually considered a central part of language documentation efforts. The field is still largely dominated by aging and poor software which clearly is not easily compatible with modern needs. Our system cannot be used offline, which is a challenge for language documentation use, but it could very well finds its place as an easy shared interface between researchers and community members.

2 Related Work

There is a myriad of active online dictionary projects targeting only one language that are under development by different people, who oftentimes are unaware of each other's contributions. In this section, we present some of the recent work on online dictionaries, which is heavily guided by the needs of one individual language. Our infrastruc-

[1]Skolt word for stream

Proceedings of the 6th International Workshop on Computational Linguistics of Uralic Languages, pages 26–30
Wien, Austria, January 10 — 11, 2020. © 2020 Association for Computational Linguistics
https://doi.org/10.18653/v1/FIXME

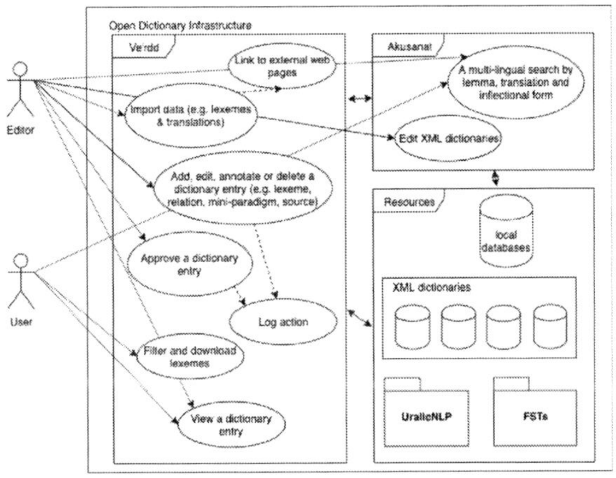

Figure 1: A UML diagram illustrating use-cases of the infrastructure

ture differs from these projects in that its driving design principle is multilinguality and support for a multitude of different Uralic languages.

A recent dictionary for St. Lawrence Island Yupik (Hunt et al., 2019) combines Foma-based morphological analyzers with an HTML based search interface. Unlike Akusanat, which does the morphological analysis and generation in the cloud, their solution runs the transducers on the client side with Foma's Javascript integration.

The Livonian dictionary consists of three databases, one – lexical, the second – morphological, and the third – a text corpus. While lemmas and their data are stored in the lexical database, and morphological forms are documented in the morphological database, all words indexed in the corpus refer to lemmas in the lexical database. Thus, all materials in the cluster can be accessed directly from the three databases (c.f. Ernštreits 2019).

There are also various attempts to build infrastructure for national majority languages. These projects also seem to be characterized by simultaneous use of different tools, with various connections to commercial software providers (see Tavast et al. 2018). Also from this point of view there is clear demand for open and easily customizable dictionary editing and data retrieval platforms, such as the infrastructure presented here.

3 The Open Dictionary Infrastructure

Akusanat is built using MediaWiki. MediaWiki is a well documented and open-source framework that comes with a set of fulfilled quality attributes such as support for multiple simultaneous users, user account management and a documented API. In addition, MediaWiki has been perceived as a useful framework for dictionaries in the past (Laxström and Kanner, 2015).

Despite the features that MediaWiki has, it does not provide an intuitive editing interface. This hinders the involvement of users of non-technical backgrounds, which is often the case for many native speakers of endangered languages. As a result, involving the native community in improving and approving the recorded information in the dictionaries is not possible. Ve′rdd is built to tackle this issue while granting users and language experts the ability to contribute to different aspects of the knowledge of such endangered languages. Additionally, Ve′rdd makes different and scattered lexicographic resources in the system available for researchers and non-academic dictionary users alike. Figure 1 shows the infrastructure of our open dictionary on a high-level of abstraction showing how different users can interact with it, revealing the interplay of the two systems: Ve′rdd and Akusanat.

3.1 Akusanat

The Akusanat dictionaries offer a distinct presentation of synchronized data shared with the Giella (Giellatekno, Divvun) infrastructure. Like the Giella dictionaries (Moshagen et al., 2014), Akusanat utilizes HFST-based (Lindén et al., 2013) finite-state transducers but with an open-source python library (UralicNLP (Hämäläinen, 2019)) in the search field, which allows users the option of entering virtually any word form to locate a possible lemma. Unlike the Giella dictionaries, however, Akusanat provides language internal links to associate words with derivational stems as well as external links to translations and cognates in other language dictionaries within Akusanat and entirely independent databases outside the domain.

The lexicographic data of Akusanat originates from the XML-based dictionaries in the Giellatekno infrastructure. Akusanat provides a user-friendly way of accessing the lexicographic data both as a regular dictionary user and as a dictionary editor solving the XML bottleneck. This means that, unlike XML, the lexicographic data can be edited simultaneously by multiple users. All the edits done in the Mediawiki-based Akusanat environment are synchronized with the XMLs residing in the Giellatekno infrastructure (c.f. Hämäläinen and Rueter 2019). However, at the same time, also editing of original XML files is possible, as the synchronization works to both directions.

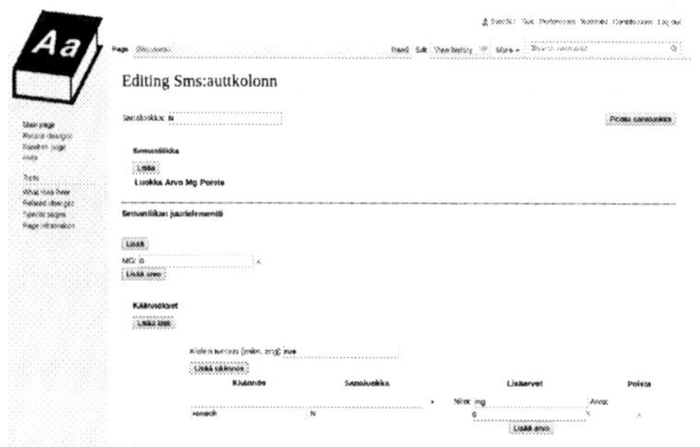

Figure 2: Edit form on Akusanat

Akusanat benefits greatly from the inbuilt quality attributes[2] of MediaWiki, such as user management, admin view, a documented Wiki-syntax and an open MediaWiki API. However, MediaWiki comes with a multitude of limitations; first and foremost, Akusanat requires a web application separate from MediaWiki to handle the synchronization of the dictionary data between the XMLs and the MediaWiki database. In addition, usability is limited by what MediaWiki has been developed for. By default, MediaWiki exposes the full Wiki syntax of each page for editing. In a dictionary setting, where the integrity of the data structure needs to be ensured, such free editing functionality has to be limited. This has been solved by introducing an edit form as seen in Figure 2. However, the more complex the demands for the system become in terms of editing, search etc., the more challenging it becomes to integrate the desired features to MediaWiki as opposed to developing a new system from scratch.

3.2 Ve′rdd

Ve′rdd is a Django-based custom developed system. The use of Django as a framework can be motivated by the fact that it scores high when compared to other popular web frameworks (Plekhanova, 2009). The goal of Ver′rdd is to correct the shortcomings of Akusanat on the intuitiveness of editing, since Akusanat users must be familiar with the structure of the XML dictionaries while editing the lexicographic entries. Ve′rdd stores information in an SQL database isolated from Akusanat which gives trusted editors the ability to perform amendments to information present in it without interfering with online dictionaries in Akusanat. Whereas Akusanat is meant to present an openly available bleeding edge version of the dictionaries, Ver′rdd, on the other hand, is tailored towards a more curated dictionary editing without immediately exposing all the edits to online users.

User experiences based on interactions with the system are continuously taken into account to facilitate the usability of the system and provide non-technical and technical users robust means for accessing and improving knowledge present in the database. Currently, the system is in use by dictionary editors authoring a Finnish-Skolt Sami dictionary and verifying the entries in it with the aim of publishing an online and a printed dictionary in early 2020. The needs of these non-technical users have been and are continuously being taken into account in the development of Ve′rdd.

Figure 1 lists the core interactions of common users (speakers or learners of the endangered language) and editors with the system. The system supports import from XML dictionaries and CSV files. Whenever data is imported, Ve′rdd consults multiple resources (e.g. Akusanat, UralicNLP and FSTs) to retrieve missing information such as part-of-speech, continuation lexica and mini-paradigms which ensures that imported information contains all the details present in other systems. Users and editors can then filter and order lexemes using multiple criteria (such as language, consonance, etc.) as seen in Figure 3.

By using Ve′rdd, editors have the ability to modify and comment on any present information in the

[2]For more discussion on quality attributes on web applications, see Offutt 2002

Figure 3: Search interface on Ve′rdd

database. To encourage the involvement of native speakers of endangered languages, especially speakers of another non-endangered language such as Russian or Finnish, the system allows approved editors with such criteria to add, edit, comment on and confirm the knowledge presented in the database. This guarantees that the information present in the system is validated and accurate as opposed to Akusanat, in which anyone can create an account and make edits. Whenever an editor performs any action (e.g. adding a lexeme or a translation), the system keeps a log which allows discovering cases of conflict and reverting back in the case of incorrect or non-verified actions are applied.

In Ve′rdd, all lexemes are stored as independent entities in the database. These independent entities are linked to each other with an abstract notion of relation. A relation between two lexemes has a direction and it can contain additional information. The system currently supports a multitude of relations such as translation, cognate or derivation. Derivational information is automatically gathered from the FSTs when data is imported to the system. An example of the relations view is show in Figure 4, the relations can be modified in their respective edit interface.

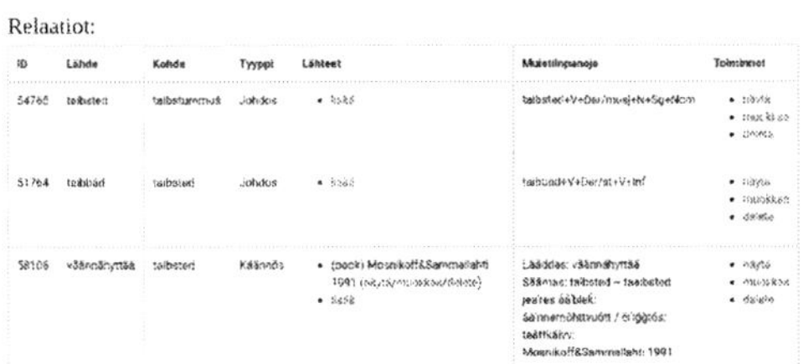

Figure 4: Relations for the word *taibsted* in Ve′rdd

For general editing, Ve′rdd exposes only the relevant information to the editor in an interface that is more narrowed down than the full-blown complexity of Akusanat edit form. Ve′rdd highlights only the essential for the dictionary editor for the particular task. This is why relations, lexemes and morphologies are edited in different interfaces; all of them accessible from the general view on the lexeme. The lexeme level editing interface is seen in Figure 5.

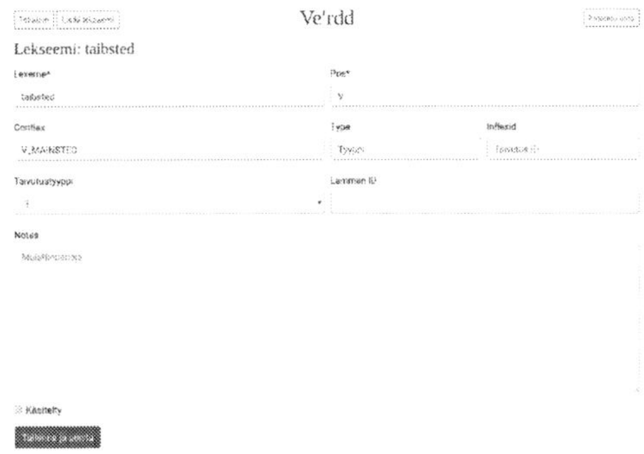

Figure 5: General edit interface for lexemes in Ve′rdd

In a timely manner, Ve′rdd can then send the approved information (by authorized experts and native speakers) to Akusanat and other resources (e.g. UralicNLP and FSTs), which would then make retaining up-to-date information across multiple resources possible; hence, reducing the risk of providing inaccurate and misleading information.

4 Discussion and Conclusions

Ve′rdd is already being used by the Skolt Sami dictionary editors as this is being written. Our development strategy involves direct interaction between the actual end users and designers, which has helped to address issues and features foreseen at the onset. A later goal would be to integrate Ve′rdd and Akusanat more completely into the infrastructure where morphological analysers and other tools are being used, so that the end-user would have a natural and intuitive environment to work with the lexicon, but so that these changes would be automatically included into the newest compiler analyzer.

More work should also be done in connecting the lexicographic resources into various corpora that are openly available. There are various ways to proceed with this: the examples could be extracted automatically, the examples could be selected with references to the corpora, or the corpora could be tagged for representative examples that would be picked into dictionary.

The most important goal in the further development of Ve′rdd must, however, be further collaboration with the users. The system will be continuously improved with the received feedback, and the user base has to be widened to encompass a larger number of users in different languages included in the project.

The source code of the systems has been made available on Bitbucket[3].

References

Rogier Blokland, Ciprian Gerstenberger, Marina Fedina, Niko Partanen, Michael Rießler, and Joshua Wilbur. 2015. Language documentation meets language technology. In Tommi A. Pirinen, Francis M. Tyers, and Trond Trosterud, editors, *First International Workshop on Computational Linguistics for Uralic Languages, 16th January, 2015, Tromsø, Norway*, number 2015:2 in Septentrio Conference Series, pages 8–18. The University Library of Tromsø.

Valts Ernštreits. 2019. Lexical tools for low-resource languages: A livonian case-study. *Electronic lexicography in the 21st century (eLex 2019): Smart lexicography*, page 103.

Benjamin Hunt, Emily Chen, Sylvia LR Schreiner, and Lane Schwartz. 2019. Community lexical access for an endangered polysynthetic language: An electronic dictionary for st. lawrence island yupik. In *Proceedings of the 2019 Conference of the North American Chapter of the Association for Computational Linguistics (Demonstrations)*, pages 122–126.

Mika Hämäläinen. 2019. UralicNLP: An NLP library for Uralic languages. *Journal of Open Source Software*, 4(37):1345.

Mika Hämäläinen and Jack Rueter. 2018. Advances in Synchronized XML-MediaWiki Dictionary Development in the Context of Endangered Uralic Languages. In *Proceedings of the Eighteenth EURALEX International Congress*, pages 967–978.

Mika Hämäläinen and Jack Rueter. 2019. An open online dictionary for endangered uralic languages. *Electronic lexicography in the 21st century (eLex 2019): Smart lexicography*.

Niklas Laxström and Antti Kanner. 2015. Multilingual semantic mediawiki for finno-ugric dictionaries. In *Septentrio Conference Series*, 2, pages 75–86.

Krister Lindén, Erik Axelson, Senka Drobac, Sam Hardwick, Juha Kuokkala, Jyrki Niemi, Tommi A Pirinen, and Miikka Silfverberg. 2013. Hfst—a system for creating nlp tools. In *International workshop on systems and frameworks for computational morphology*, pages 53–71. Springer.

[3]https://bitbucket.org/mokha/verdd/src/master/ and https://bitbucket.org/mikahama/saame/src/master/

Sjur Moshagen, Jack Rueter, Tommi Pirinen, Trond Trosterud, and Francis M. Tyers. 2014. Open-Source Infrastructures for Collaborative Work on Under-Resourced Languages. In *The LREC 2014 Workshop "CCURL 2014 - Collaboration and Computing for Under-Resourced Languages in the Linked Open Data Era"*, pages 71–77.

Jeff Offutt. 2002. Quality attributes of web software applications. *IEEE software*, 19(2):25–32.

Julia Plekhanova. 2009. Evaluating web development frameworks: Django, ruby on rails and cakephp. *Institute for Business and Information Technology*.

Arvi Tavast, Margit Langemets, Jelena Kallas, and Kristina Koppel. 2018. Unified data modelling for presenting lexical data: The case of ekilex. In *Ed. J. Čibej, V. Gorjanc, I. Kosem & Simon Krek, Proceedings of the XVIII EURALEX International Congress: EURALEX: Lexicography in Global Contexts, Ljubljana*, pages 749–761.

Рохир Блокланд, Михаэль Рийсслер [Рисслер], Нико Партанен, Марина Федина, and Андрей Чемышев. 2014. Использование цифровых корпусов и компьютерных програм в диалектологических исследованиях. pages 252–255. ИИЯЛ УНЦ РАН.

Towards a Speech Recognizer for Komi, an Endangered and Low-Resource Uralic Language

Nils Hjortnæs
Department of Linguistics
Indiana University
Bloomington, IN
nhjortn@iu.edu

Niko Partanen
University of Helsinki
Helsinki, Finland
niko.partanen@helsinki.fi

Michael Rießler
University of Eastern Finland
Joensuu, Finland
michael.riessler@uef.fi

Francis M. Tyers
Department of Linguistics
Indiana University
Bloomington, IN
ftyers@iu.edu

Abstract

In this paper, we present and evaluate a first pass speech recognition model for Komi, an endangered and low-resource Uralic language spoken in Russia. We compare a transfer learning approach from English with a baseline model trained from scratch using DeepSpeech (an end-to-end ASR model) and evaluate the impact of fine tuning a language model for correcting the output of the network. We also provides an overview of previous research and perform an error analysis with a focus on the language model and the challenges introduced by a fieldwork based corpus. Though we only achieve a 70.9% Character Error Rate, there is a great deal to be learned from the circumstances presented by our data's structure and origins.

1 Introduction

In the creation of any corpus of spoken text, the transcription work can be identified as the major bottleneck that limits how much recorded speech data can be annotated and included in the corpus. The situation is particularly dire with endangered languages for which language technology does not exist (Foley et al., 2018, 206). But typically, even corpus building projects working with spoken data from majority languages manage to transcribe and analyze only a fraction of the materials for which they have recorded audio data. The need for speech-to-text tools is not restricted to fieldwork-based language documentation producing new speech recordings, but rather a continuum of projects and languages with various levels of resources. There is also an immense build-up of non-transcribed legacy audio recordings of endangered languages stored at various private or institutional archives, in which case even a small and endangered language may have a significant amount of currently unused materials. At the same time, speech recognition technologies have been fully functional for a variety of languages for some time already. Although the use of such tools would potentially offer large improvements for language documentation and corpus building, it is still unclear how to integrate this technology into work with endangered languages in the most successful manner.

Spoken corpora of endangered languages for the study of endangered languages are often relatively small, especially when compared to the resources available for larger languages. This is not necessarily due to lack of relevant audio recordings. There are no statistics about the typical sizes of endangered language corpora, but it can be assumed that transcribed portions are somewhere from a few hours to tens of hours, with magnitudes of hundreds of hours becoming rare. This is much lower than the threshold usually estimated that is needed for major speech recognition systems. From this point of view, the initial goal of using speech recognition in this context could be attempting to improve the transcription speed. This would result in larger transcribed corpora which could continuously improve the speech recognition system. The accuracy needed to reach that point would be such that it is faster to correct than do transcription manually, as before then speech recognition doesn't help the tran-

Proceedings of the 6th International Workshop on Computational Linguistics of Uralic Languages, pages 31–37
Wien, Austria, January 10 — 11, 2020.
https://doi.org/10.18653/v1/FIXME

scription task.

2 Related work

There have been several earlier attempts to build pipelines that integrate speech recognition into language documentation context, most importantly Elpis (Foley et al., 2019) and Persephone (Adams et al., 2018). These systems are still maturing, with desire to make them more easily available for an ordinary linguist with no technical background in speech recognition. There are only individual reports of project having yet adapted these tools, with exceptions such as work described in Michaud et al. (2018) on the Na language, where an error rate of 17% was reported. Also Adams et al. (2018) report that it seems possible to achieve phoneme error rates below 30% with only half an hour of recordings. Both of these experiments were done in a single speaker setting.

Instead of using tools specifically designed in a language documentation context, in this paper we train and evaluate a speech recognition system for Zyrian Komi using DeepSpeech (Hannun et al., 2014).

DeepSpeech has been used previously with a variety of languages. It is most commonly used with large languages when the resources available vastly outnumber what we have. We found several other cases where DeepSpeech was used, for example, with Russian (Iakushkin et al., 2018), Romanian (Panaite et al., 2019), Tujian (Yu et al., 2019) and Bangla (Saurav et al., 2018). All of these experiments report higher scores than we do, with the exception of Russian, with smaller data, but there are important differences as well. Romanian recordings were done in studio environment, Tujian sentences were specifically translated to Chinese to take advantage of the Chinese model, and Bangla experiment had a limited vocabulary. The Russian corpus has well over 1000 hours, which brings it, in a way, out of the low-resource scenario where the other mentioned works took place.

One experiment with DeepSpeech that seems particularly relevant to us is the work done recently on Seneca (Jimerson et al., 2018) because the word error rate was very high and difficult to reduce.

The overview of related work leads us to the conclusion that speech recognition has reached significant results in conditions where very large transcribed datasets are available, or there are other constraints present, such as a small number of speakers and/or studio recording quality.

3 Komi language

Komi is a Uralic language spoken primarily in the North-Eastern corner of European Russia, bordering the Ural mountains in the East. There are, however, numerous settlements where Komi is spoken outside the main speaking areas, and these communities span from the Kola Peninsula to Western Siberia.

Zyrian Komi is closely related to Permian and Jazva Komi. All Komi varieties are mutually intelligible and form a complex dialect continuum. Komi is more distantly related to Udmurt, which is spoken south from main Komi areas. Together Komi and Udmurt form the Permic branch of Uralic languages. Other languages in this family are significantly more distantly related.

The Komi language currently has approximately 160,000 speakers, and it is spoken in a large number of individual settlements in Northern Russia. The language is taught, although to a limited degree, in schools as a subject in some municipalities. There are several weekly publications and the written language is stable and generally well known. There is also continuous online presence. The largest Komi corpus contains over 50 million words (Fu-Lab, 2019). For a more thorough description see, i.e. Hausenberg; Цыпанов (2009).

Komi is spoken in intensive contact with Russian, a dominant Slavic language of the region. A large portion of the Komi lexicon is borrowed from Russian, and virtually all speakers are currently bilingual. Bilingual phenomena present in contemporary Komi have been studied in detail (Leinonen, 2002, 2006), and with particularly importance for our study, the northern dialect that is predominantly present in our corpus is known for its extensive Russian contact (Leinonen, 2009).

Komi is written with Cyrillic orthography. The script is essentially phonemic, although different character combinations are used to represent similar sounds in different contexts, as is typical for Cyrillic scripts.

4 Resources used

4.1 The Spoken Komi Corpus

The majority of Komi resources used in this study originate from the Kone Foundation funded *Iźva Komi Documentation Project*, the results of which are currently available in the Language Bank of Finland (Blokland et al., 2019). However, there are numerous Komi materials that are in various stages of being turned into corpora, and these include recordings stored in the Institute for the Languages of Finland. Eventually all these materials should be combined into the Spoken Komi Corpus, and developing speech recognition technologies that can operate on various recording types is an important part in advancing the work on these resources.

The corpus is relatively large, containing around 35 hours of transcribed utterances. The number of total recorded hours is much higher, as this count includes only the transcribed segments without silences. Also the number of individual speakers is very high, at over 200. This has been made possible by systematic inclusion of archival data, as the goal has been to build a corpus that is representative from different periods from which we have recordings, and also so that different geographical areas would be evenly covered.

Specific features of the corpus are that the majority of content consists of conversations between two or more native speakers. These conversations have been arranged in an interview-like setting, so one of the participant is leading the conversation with questions on various topics. The transcriptions are done by native Komi speakers, and have been systematically revised by one additional native speaking project participant besides the person who did the transcription. The recordings are very accurate in that small primary interjections such as 'mm' and 'aha' are transcribed. There is also a large amount of overlapping speech.

The transcriptions are in a Cyrillic writing system that follows the rules of Komi orthography. A similar system has been used in a recent Komi dialect dictionary (Безносикова et al., 2012). This convention was selected for various reasons, both practical and methodological. Having the results of language documentation work in written standard, when it exists, makes the work accessible for the community and allows better integration of language technology (Gerstenberger et al., 2017a,b). This is also obvious with the current study, as the speech recognition system that operates with the orthography is arguably more useful for the community than one which outputs a transcription system that only specialists in the field can easily understand. That being said, the use of orthography also makes some tasks such as speech recognition harder, as the phoneme-to-grapheme correspondence is less transparent.

Portion	**Clips**	**Duration (Hours:Minutes)**
train	37043	27:50
dev	4756	3:33
test	4736	3:28
Total:	46535	34:51

Table 1: Statistics on the training data

The texts in the corpus have been manually segmented into utterances and transcribed in ELAN. These segments have been transformed into pairs of audio and plain text files. For loading into DeepSpeech, the audio samples have been normalized for length such that clips over 10 seconds, DeepSpeech's default cutoff, are excluded.

4.2 DeepSpeech

DeepSpeech (Hannun et al., 2014) is a relatively simple Recurrent Neural Network designed specifically for the task of Speech Recognition. It has since been updated and made available[1]. The biggest change between the current 0.5.1 release of DeepSpeech and the original is the switch to an LSTM instead of an RNN. In addition, some hyperparameters have been updated. Unless otherwise noted, we use the default parameters in the 0.5.1 release.

Figure 1 outlines the structure of the DeepSpeech Neural Network. The feature extraction is a mapping of characters to the nominal values 1-N where N is the length of the set of characters appearing in the data. This is followed by three fully connected ReLU layers, the LSTM layer, and a final ReLU layer. All layers have a width of 2048. The sixth layer is a softmax layer with a width determined by the length of the alphabet.

The final step of DeepSpeech is correction using a language model (lm), which allows us to calculate the probability of a given character sequence. It is integrated into DeepSpeech by balancing the probability of the neural network's output with the probability of a character sequence in the lm (Hannun et al., 2014). The hyper-parameter alpha controls the degree to which the language model edits the neural network's output and the hyper-parameter beta controls the cost of inserting word breaks. A

[1]https://github.com/mozilla/DeepSpeech/releases/tag/v0.5.1

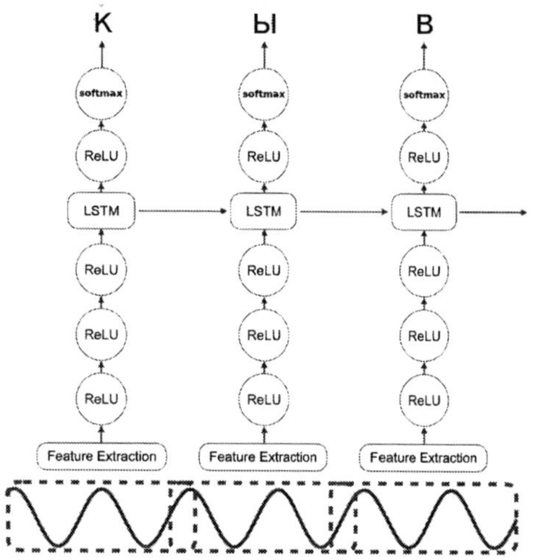

Figure 1: The architecture of Mozilla's DeepSpeech (Meyer, 2019)

higher alpha favors language model editing and a higher beta favors inserting word breaks.

5 Experiment

To pre-process the data, we shuffled it and split it into an 8-1-1 ration of training, testing, and development. We then created an alphabet of characters and symbols which appear in the text, the length of which determines the width of the output layer of the DeepSpeech neural network.

As a baseline, we trained DeepSpeech using the default parameters, except for batch sizes, on the Komi corpus from scratch. We then trained a transfer learning model on DeepSpeech, again with the default parameters except batch sizes, for comparison. Rather than using the default batch size of 1 for train, test, and dev, we used 128, 32, and 32 respectively for all experiments. Finally, we tuned the learning rate at factors of 10 from 0.001 to 0.000001 and dropouts of 5, 10, and 15%.

We trained the transfer learning model using the transfer_learning2[2] branch of DeepSpeech. This branch allows you to cut off the last N layers of the network and reinitialize them from scratch. This is necessary for the final layer because the alphabet, and therefore the width of the final output layer, will almost certainly change. Meyer (2019) found that cutting off two layers and transferring four when using DeepSpeech, as well as allowing fine-tuning of the transferred layers, provides the best boost in performance. We therefore follow suit, and cut off two layers and allow fine-tuning for our transfer models. For convenience, we used English as the source language because it ships with DeepSpeech and is known to have good results. Languages with comparable performance which are historically related to Komi, such as the main contact language Russian, provide potential avenues of research worth further experimentation.

A language model is a critical piece of DeepSpeech because it corrects for the fact that every character in the orthography is not pronounced in natural speech. We generated out n-gram trie language model, as in Hannun et al. (2014), using kenlm (Heafield, 2011) with the default parameters. Because a language model is trained on unlabeled text, we can train it on a much larger corpus than the speech dataset. Our corpus is composed of several books, newspaper articles, an old Wikipedia dump, and the Komi Republic website. These are all in the standard, modern Zyrian orthography. We found that the quantity of data provided by these various sources was more effective than using the transcriptions from our data.

Because the language model is applied to the output of the neural network, it can be tuned separately. Therefore, in the interest of time, we trained the network with the default language model hyperparameters of 0.75 and 1.85 for alpha and beta respectively. We then tuned the language model on the output from the best neural network for the baseline, transfer learning baseline, and tuned models. We tuned the lm for alphas of 0.25, 0.50, and 0.75 and betas of 1, 3, 5, 7, and 9, as can be seen in Tables 3 and 4.

In order to see whether the language model was helping or hindering our performance, we set both alpha and beta to 0, effectively disabling the influence of the language model entirely. This also allowed us to check the output of the neural network directly, as this also disabled the insertion of word breaks.

6 Results

The best results were achieved using the transfer learning model with a learning rate of 0.00001 and dropout of 10%. Early stopping was disabled as it is very aggressive, and all other parameters were the default or the batch sizes stated above as of release 0.5.1.

[2] https://github.com/mozilla/DeepSpeech/tree/transfer-learning2

System	**CER** (%)	**WER** (%)
Baseline	82.7	99.1
Transfer tuned	72.1	100.0
Transfer baseline	82.9	**98.3**
Baseline tuned lm	73.8	100.0
Baseline no lm	72.7	100.0
Transfer no lm	**70.9**	100.0

Table 2: The best results for our baseline and transfer learning models without tuning the language model, with tuning, and without a language model

Table 2 compares the best scores achieved for the baseline and transfer models under different conditions. The transfer models perform better under all respective conditions, but the baseline model outperforms the baseline transfer model when tuned. While tuning clearly has an effect on the Character Error Rate, the tuned models were unable to accurately recognize any full words. An error analysis showed that the words the baseline models were capturing are short filler words rather than content or even common function words. This is further discussed below.

Table 3 and Table 4 show the impact of the language model on the accuracy of the speech recognition system. A higher alpha favors correcting the output of the neural network with the language model, and a higher beta favors inserting word breaks. We see in both tables that a lower alpha achieves better results, corroborating Table 2, where disabling the language model achieved the best results. As alpha increases, the best results are achieved with increasing beta values as well.

7 Discussion

These preliminary results show that transfer learning is a promising avenue for developing a speech recognition system for documentary audio data. While the gain is small as compared to the baseline, any improvement in the network will help the language model better predict the true orthography. In addition, we found that the transfer model predicts slightly more sensible guesses than the baseline, even if it is not reflected in the error rates. For example, (1) and (3) are produced by the baseline and (2) and (4) are produced by the transfer model. Despite the overall error rate being high, both of these pairs of examples indicate that the potential for improvement is there, and that transfer learning is slightly more accurate.

(1) но печера ю вылын
 н п зино юн

(2) но печера ю вылын
 ино ече ю н

(3) но ме же том на
 н м же м

(4) но ме же том на
 н не же т

A negative indication of potential, however, is that several of the examples which are boosting the CER in particular are filler words such as *но*, *мм*, or *и*. That DeepSpeech is only good at identifying these exceptionally simple examples with a high degree of accuracy could be an indication of a class imbalance problem where the simple, small examples become too ingrained in the network and prevent more complex, more desirable behavior from emerging. For example, in (5), *но* and *и* appear in the output despite having no correlate in the source text.

(5) передовик вӧлэма
 и ец теф и техо пняе но

DeepSpeech has built-in mechanisms for validating data before it is used, including skipping samples deemed too long or too short. For short audio clips, however, the threshold is fairly lenient. For this experiment, only two samples out of the 47232 were excluded for being too short. By increasing the minimum length of the audio clip for it to be valid, we can ignore these confounding data points and potentially improve the quality of the speech recognition.

Another way to refine the dataset would be to selectively choose data generated by certain speakers, such as those who contributed most to the corpus. As previously mentioned, there are over 200 speakers who have contributed to this corpus, but most of them are only a small portion. While this does decrease the potential for robustness when developing a generalized speech recognition system, it is less of an issue when considering the integration of speech recognition into field work and documentation, as there tend to be few consultants providing large quantities of data each. This would also decrease our total quantity of data, but others have been successful using methods similar to those

	CER/WER	beta 1	3	5	7	9
alpha	0.25	77.3/100.0	74.9/100.0	**73.8**/100.0	74.5/100.0	78.2/100.0
	0.5	80.7/100.0	77.7/100.0	75.2/100.0	74.3/100.0	75.0/100.0
	0.75	84.1/**98.6**	80.7/100.0	77.8/100.0	75.7/100.0	74.8/100.0

Table 3: The impact of tuning the language model parameters on Character and Word Error Rates for the baseline model.

	CER/WER	beta 1	3	5	7	9
alpha	0.25	76.6/100.0	73.2/100.0	**72.1**/100.0	74.0/100.0	81.8/100.0
	0.5	81.0/99.4	77.0/100.0	74.0/100.0	73.3/100.0	75.8/100.0
	0.75	85.2/**98.1**	80.1/100.0	77.2/100.0	74.8/100.0	74.7/100.0

Table 4: The impact of tuning the language model parameters on Character and Word Error Rates for the transfer learning model.

we outline above on smaller datasets (Meyer, 2019; Jimerson et al., 2018; Panaite et al., 2019; Yu et al., 2019).

The results in Table 2 show that the language model needs refinement, as it currently hinders rather than helps the performance of the system. The initial lm was trained on the training data from our corpus, and performed even worse than the current one. The current lm is assembled from a mix of domains from several time periods, which may be one explanation for its poor performance. However, tables 3 and 4 show that tuning the language model parameters is still important, and also indicate good parameters for training the neural network, as the language model is used for validation on the dev set.

8 Possible ELAN integration

Although the accuracy is at the moment rather low, it's worth considering how speech recognition technology could in principle be integrated into language documentation work. Previous work of (Gerstenberger et al., 2017a) presents a very effective approach to integrate a morphological analyser into ELAN through an external Python script, and there is no reason why speech recognition could not be implemented in similar fashion. The task may be computationally more complex, but if the speech recognition system is trained on individual utterances, it should always be possible to send such utterances as input to the system, and to predict their transcriptions.

From this point of view the most straightforward way to use speech recognition in this context could be to manually segment the ELAN file, as one normally does in manual workflows, and predict the transcription on each of those segments individually. In this paper we have only focused on the problem of speech recognition itself, but actually executing speech recognition on a new audio file involves segmentation and speaker diarization, both of which are complex and, to some degree, unsolved problems.

9 Conclusion & Further Work

The most central upcoming task is to repeat the experiment with other speech recognition systems that are currently available. Other potential lines of research would be to repeat this experiment with comparable datasets on other languages, in order to see whether the challenges reported in this paper are more connected to features of Komi dataset, or if they relate more to DeepSpeech infrastructure.

Meanwhile, there are also several things we can do towards improving the results on Komi. As several projects did report successful experiments when training on data that contains only an individual speaker, it seems logical to select only those speakers who contribute most to our corpus in the future, and retrain the system individually on that data. Similarly, simplifying the set of speakers such as male or female speakers only may have a similar effect.

Acknowledgments

Niko Partanen and Michael Rießler collaborate within the project Language Documentation meets Language Technology: The Next Step in the Description of Komi, funded by the Kone Foundation, Finland.

This research was supported in part by Lilly Endowment, Inc., through its support for the Indiana University Pervasive Technology Institute.

References

Oliver Adams, Trevor Cohn, Graham Neubig, Hilaria Cruz, Steven Bird, and Alexis Michaud. 2018. Evaluating phonemic transcription of low-resource tonal languages for language documentation.

Rogier Blokland, Marina Fedina, Niko Partanen, and Michael Rießler. 2019. Spoken komi corpus. the language bank of finland version 1.0.0.

Ben Foley, Joshua T Arnold, Rolando Coto-Solano, Gautier Durantin, T Mark Ellison, Daan van Esch, Scott Heath, Frantisek Kratochvil, Zara Maxwell-Smith, David Nash, et al. 2018. Building speech recognition systems for language documentation: The coedl endangered language pipeline and inference system (elpis). In *SLTU*, pages 205–209.

Ben Foley, Alina Rakhi, Nicholas Lambourne, Nicholas Buckeridge, and Janet Wiles. 2019. Elpis, an accessible speech-to-text tool. *Proc. Interspeech 2019*, pages 4624–4625.

Fu-Lab. 2019. Корпус коми языка.

Ciprian Gerstenberger, Niko Partanen, and Michael Rießler. 2017a. Instant annotations in elan corpora of spoken and written komi, an endangered language of the barents sea region. In *Proceedings of the 2nd Workshop on the Use of Computational Methods in the Study of Endangered Languages*, pages 57–66.

Ciprian Gerstenberger, Niko Partanen, and Michael Rießler. 2017b. Instant annotations in ELAN corpora of spoken and written Komi, an endangered language of the Barents Sea region. In *Proceedings of the 2nd Workshop on the Use of Computational Methods in the Study of Endangered Languages*, pages 57–66, Honolulu. Association for Computational Linguistics.

Awni Hannun, Carl Case, Jared Casper, Bryan Catanzaro, Greg Diamos, Erich Elsen, Ryan Prenger, Sanjeev Satheesh, Shubho Sengupta, Adam Coates, and Andrew Y. Ng. 2014. Deep speech: Scaling up end-to-end speech recognition.

Anu-Reet Hausenberg. Komi. In Daniel Abondolo, editor, *The Uralic languages*, pages 305–326. Routledge.

Kenneth Heafield. 2011. Kenlm: Faster and smaller language model queries. In *Proceedings of the sixth workshop on statistical machine translation*, pages 187–197. Association for Computational Linguistics.

OO Iakushkin, GA Fedoseev, AS Shaleva, AB Degtyarev, and OS Sedova. 2018. Russian-language speech recognition system based on deepspeech.

Robbie Jimerson, Kruthika Simha, Raymond W Ptucha, and Emily Prudhommeaux. 2018. Improving ASR output for endangered language documentation. In *SLTU*, pages 187–191.

Marja Leinonen. 2002. Influence of Russian on the syntax of Komi. 57:195–358.

Marja Leinonen. 2006. The russification of Komi. Number 27 in Slavica Helsingiensia, pages 234–245. Helsinki University Press.

Marja Leinonen. 2009. Russian influence on the Ižma Komi dialect. *International Journal of Bilingualism*, 13(2):309–329.

Josh Meyer. 2019. Multi-task and transfer learning in low-resource speech recognition.

Alexis Michaud, Oliver Adams, Trevor Anthony Cohn, Graham Neubig, and Séverine Guillaume. 2018. Integrating automatic transcription into the language documentation workflow: Experiments with Na data and the Persephone toolkit.

Marilena Panaite, Stefan Ruseti, Mihai Dascalu, and Stefan Trausan-Matu. 2019. Towards a Deep Speech model for Romanian language. In *2019 22nd International Conference on Control Systems and Computer Science (CSCS)*, pages 416–419. IEEE.

Jillur Rahman Saurav, Shakhawat Amin, Shafkat Kibria, and M Shahidur Rahman. 2018. Bangla speech recognition for voice search. In *2018 International Conference on Bangla Speech and Language Processing (ICBSLP)*, pages 1–4. IEEE.

Chongchong Yu, Yunbing Chen, Yueqiao Li, Meng Kang, Shixuan Xu, and Xueer Liu. 2019. Cross-language end-to-end speech recognition research based on transfer learning for the low-resource Tujia language. *Symmetry*, 11(2):179.

ЛМ Безносикова, ЕА Айбабина, НК Забоева, and РИ Коснырева. 2012. Коми сёрнисикас кывчукӧр. Словарь диалектов коми языка: в 2-х томах/ИЯЛИ Коми НЦ УрО РАН; под ред. ЛМ Безносиковой.

Йӧлгинь Цыпанов. 2009. Перым кывъяслӧн талунъя серпас. *Suomalais-Ugrilaisen Seuran Toimituksia = Mémoires de la Société Finno-Ougrienne*, 258:191–206.

Hunting for antiharmonic stems in Erzya

Fejes, László
Research Institute for Linguistics
†Hungarian Academy of Sciences
fejes.laszlo@gmail.com

Abstract

This paper presents a research study aimed to clarify whether there are antiharmonic stems in Modern Standard Erzya. At least two types of Erzya stems more or less liable to antiharmony were identified using the material of an Erzya dictionary and Internet search.

A cikk egy olyan kutatást mutat be, mely azt kívánta tisztázni, hogy vannak-e antiharmonikus tövek a mai sztenderd erzában. Egy erza szótár anyaga és internetes keresés alapján két olyan tőtípust sikerült azonosítani, mely kisebb-nagyobb mértékben hajlamos az antiharmóniára.

1 Introduction

In the literature on Erzya phonology, we usually find that Erzya has vowel harmony (Бондарко and Полякова 1993, 94–95; Keresztes 1990, 37; Keresztes 2011, 22-23; Bartens 1999, 66–67). However, suffix alternations due to harmony rather suggest that Erzya has vowel-consonant harmony. To our knowledge, the question of antiharmony in Erzya has never been discussed in the literature.

In Section 1, the notion of harmony, disharmony and antiharmony will be defined. The basic regularities of Erzya[1] harmony will be presented as well. It will be determined what kind of stems must be considered antiharmonic in Erzya.

In Section 2, a test on the material of an Erzya dictionary will be presented. Using a Perl script, word forms which show the symptoms of antiharmony were collected. Their antihamonic behavior was certified also by tests via Google[2]. It will be defined in phonological terms what kind of stems may be antiharmonic.

In Section 3, the result of another **test** via Google will be presented: some stems, the antiharmonicity of which could not be tested automatically in the dictionary material, will be tested with some forms expectedly occuring on the Internet.

2 Harmony, disharmony and antiharmony in Erzya

2.1 Harmony, disharmony and antiharmony in general

Harmony is a phenomenon according to which in a given language, phonemes belong to two groups the members of which cannot occur together in a given domain (typically inside a word). These groups are usually devided by some phonetical feature. For example, in Finnish, Hungarian, Hill Mari or Turkish, front and back vowels do not typically occur in the same word form. However, there can be phonemes which do not belong to either of these classes, i.e. they can occur together with the phonemes of both harmonic classes inside the domain: these are called neutrals.

The most evident sign of neutrality is the behaviour of the phoneme in suffixes: neutrals do not alternate due to harmony. For example, in Finnish and Hill Mari, /i/ and /e/[3] never alternate with other vowels due to vowel harmony. However, their behavior is different: Finnish neutral vowels are transparent (the backness or frontness of the vowel after them is identical with the backness or frontness

[1] In the following, the term *Erzya* should be understood as Modern Standard Erzya. From the point of view of harmony, Erzya dialects can strongly differ from each other.

[2] One of my reviewers disapproves of the use of Google and warns me that I ignore (Kilgarriff, 2007). Nonetheless, since I do not deal with statistics based on Google data, Kilgarriff's criticism does not apply to this study. I use Google solely to find a given form and do not deal with its frequency.

[3] Also /i:/ and /e:/; since the length is never relevant, phonemes differing only in lenght will not be differentiated.

Proceedings of the 6th International Workshop on Computational Linguistics of Uralic Languages, pages 38–47
Wien, Austria, January 10 — 11, 2020. © 2020 Association for Computational Linguistics
https://doi.org/10.18653/v1/FIXME

of the vowel before them), while Hill Mari neutral vowels are opaque (there must be a front vowel after them, due to the fact that they are front vowels). Neutrality can sometimes be gradual, as in Hungarian. Usually /i/[4], /eː/ and /ɛ/ are considered to be neutrals. High /i/, despite some special exceptions, does not alternate in suffixes due to harmony; mid /eː/ alternates with /ɑː/ in approximatelly half of the suffixes (but not in the other half); low /ɛ/ practically always alternates with /ɒ/ or /o/ (and, in the latter case, also with /ø/). In a similar way, /i/ is always transparent (although two /i/s following each other morpheme-internally can also be opaque, c. f. /ɒli-nɒk/ 'Ali-DAT' but /ɒlibi-nɒk/ ~ /ɒlibi-nɛk/ 'alibi-DAT'), /eː/ and /ɛ/ can be both opaque and transparent, although /eː/ is always transparent in some stems (/kɒʃteːj-nɒk/, but */kɒʃteːj-nɛk/ 'manor-DAT'), and /ɛ/ is always opaque in some stems (/oktoːbɛr-nɛk/, but */oktoːbɛr-nɒk/ 'October-DAT'). Turkish has no neutral vowels.

Forms containing phonemes that belong to different harmonic classes (such as Finnish /ɑmɑtøːri/ or Hungarian /ɒmɒtøːr/ 'amateur') are called *disharmonic*. Sometimes even forms with both back harmonic and phonetically front neutral phonemes phonetically (such as Finnish /kone/ 'machine' or Hungarian /loːveː/ 'money (coll.)') are called disharmonic.

In languages with harmony, stems containing only neutral phonemes take suffixes according to their phonetic value (e. g. stems with phonetically front neutrals take the front allophones of harmonic suffixes), e. g. Finnish /vede-sːæ/ and not */vede-sːɑ/ 'water-INE', Hungarian /viːz-bɛn/ and not */viːz-bɒn/ 'water-INE'. However, there can be exceptions.

In Hungarian, there are also stems, which despite that they contain phonetically front neutral vowels, always take back variants of suffixes. These stems are called *antiharmonic*. Moreover, there is at least one class which is regularly antiharmonic: verbs containing /iː/, except for /t͡ʃiːp/ 'nip, peck, burn (food)', always take the back allomorph of harmonic suffixes: /iːr-ok/ 'write-1SG' (c. f. /iːr-ɛk/ 'Irish-PL'). Antiharmony is very rare with stems containing /eː/ (/t͡seːl-ok/, but */t͡seːl-ɛk/ 'target-PL'; /heːj-ak/, but */heːj-ɛk/ 'peel-PL') or /ɛ/ (/ʃva(ː)jc-bɒn ~ /ʃvɛjc-bɒn/ ~ /ʃvɛjc-bɛn/ 'Switzerland-INE', /ʃpa(ː)jz-bɒn ~ /ʃpɛjz-bɒn/ ~ /ʃpɛjz-bɛn/ 'pantry-INE'). As the examples show, in the last cases there is an /a(ː)/ : /ɛ/ alternation in the stem and that evokes vacillation in suffixation. Historically the case of /heːj/ 'peel' is similar, since it is etymologically identical with /hɒj/ 'hair'.

[4] Also /iː/; when the length is not relevant, the two phonemes will not be differentiated.

Antiharmonic stems in Hungarian except for some marginal examples (/dɛreːk/ 'waist' : /dɛreːk-nɒk/ 'waist-DAT' : /dɛrɛk-ɒt/ 'waist-ACC'; /piʃil-ek/ ~ playfull (dialectal?) /piʃil-ok/ 'pee-1SG'.

On the contrary, Finnish has no antiharmonic stems. In Hungarian, antiharmonic stems are always suffixed by the back variants of suffixes (and vacillating stems can be suffixed by both the back and the front allomorph of the suffix). There are no such stems in Finnish, but two stems are suffixed by an antiharmonic allomorph of one and the same inflectional suffix: /mer-tɑ/, but */mer-tæ/ 'see-PART', /ver-tɑ/ , but */ver-tæ/ 'see-PART'. The phenomenon is much more general in derivation, see e. g. /kiːt-os/ 'thanks' from /kiːtːæ-/ 'to thank', /itku/ 'cry(ing)' from /itke-/ 'to cry, to weep' etc. (c. f. Hakulinen et al. 2004, §16).

In general, we must conclude that antiharmonic stems are those stems which are not suffixed by the allomorphs we would expect by the regularities of harmony in the given language, but those allomorphs which are unexpected.

2.2 Harmony in Erzya

Erzya has five vowels: /i/, /e/, /ɑ/, /o/ and /u/. Out of these only /e/ and /o/ alternate with each other due to harmony (see below), therefore, the other three must be considered neutrals. However, all the neutrals are opaque: if the vowel after them is a mid one, /i/ must be followed by /e/, /ɑ/ and /u/ must be followed by /o/ – at least in suffixation. Nonetheless, these rules can be overriden by consonants.

In Erzya harmony, consonants also play a key role. Dental consonants can be arranged into non-palatalized vs. palatalized pairs: /t/ vs. /tʲ/, /d/ vs. /dʲ/, /s/ vs. /sʲ/, /z/ vs. /zʲ/, /t͡s/ vs. /t͡sʲ/, /n/ vs. /nʲ/, /l/ vs. /lʲ/, and /r/ vs. /rʲ/. Stem-final palatalized consonants and the palatal /j/ trigger the use of front allomorphs of suffixes alternating due to harmony, independently of the quality of the last vowel in the stem. Therefore, Erzya "vowel harmony" should be considered vowel-consonant harmony.

With non-dental consonants, palatality plays no phonological role: however, phonetically they are palatalized in a palatal environment (before front vowels or palatalized dentals or /j/). According to

(Keresztes, 1990, 25) and (Keresztes, 2011, 18), all consonants other than dentals are alternated allophonically, although there are only labial and velar examples given. Bartens (1999, 27) states that only labials and velars have palatalized allophones before front vowels. Имайкина (1996, 9) claims that alveaolars /ʒ/, /ʃ/ and /t͡ʃ/ are always "hard", that is they are never palatalized.

Based on Keresztes (1990, 37) and Keresztes (2011, 22–23), the following suffixation types can be distinguished from the point of view of harmony:

- Both triggers and targets are vowels: /kudo-so-nzo/ 'house-INE-3SG' : /vel^{j}e-se-nze/ 'village-S3-INE';
- Both triggers and targets are consonants: /kɑl-t/ 'fish-PL' : /kɑl^{j}-t^{j}/ 'willow-PL';
- Triggers are vowels and targets are both vowels and consonants: /kudo-vtomo/ 'house-ABE' : /vel^{j}e-vt^{j}eme/ 'village-ABE';
- Triggers are consonants and targets are both vowels and consonants: /kɑl-do/ 'fish-ABL' : /kɑl^{j}-d^{j}e/ 'willow-ABL';
- Triggers are vowels but targets are consonants: /kudo-t/ 'house-PL' : /vel^{j}e-t^{j}/ 'village-PL';
- Triggers are consonants but targets are vowels: /kɑl-so/ 'fish-INE' : /kɑl^{j}-se/ 'willow-INE'.

It seems that sibilants and affricates (and consonant clusters including them) are never targets of harmony.

Since stem-internal (dis)harmony is not relevant from the point of view of antiharmony, it will be not discussed here. Let it be enough that there is no strict harmony inside stems.

2.3 Antiharmony in Erzya

The basic rules of Erzya suffixation due to harmony are quite simple: if the last vowel of the stem is front or the stem-final consonant is palatalized, the front (palatalized) variant of the harmonizing suffix must be chosen. In all other cases, the back (non-palatalized) variant of the harmonizing suffix must be chosen.

Since antiharmonic stems are those which do not choose the expected suffix allomorph, stems must be considered antiharmonic if:

- the last vowel of the stem is front and/or the stem-final dental is palatalized, but the stem is suffixed by the back (non-palatalized) variant of harmonizing suffixes;
- or the last vowel of the stem is back and the stem-final dental (if there is one) is not palatalized, but the stem is suffixed by the front (palatalized) variant of harmonizing suffixes.

The problem is how to find these stems (if they exist at all).

3 Looking for the antiharmonic stems

Since native speakers use their language unconsciously, they cannot elicit antiharmonic stems. However, they can notice that some stems are suffixed in an unexpected way when hearing slips of the tongue or when there are dialectal differences in the harmonic and antiharmonic suffixation of the same stems.

L2 learners are more probable to notice these irregularities when they try to suffix the stems due to the learned rules but native speakers consider the given form incorrect. However, they can meet suffixed forms from which they can learn which set of suffixes must be used with the stem without noticing these are irregular in a way.

By automatic parsing, it seems to be practically impossible to find antiharmonic stems in morphologically unanalysed texts. On the contrary, antiharmonic stems must pop up during the development of automatic morphological analyzers, since the suffixed forms of antiharmonic stems cannot be analyzed in the regular way. Although Erzya morphological analyzers exist,[5] to our knowledge, no findings were reported on antiharmonic stems.

The research to be presented here was conducted on data from an Erzya–Hungarian dictionary (Mészáros and Sirmankine, 2003). The choice of the research material was determined by the fact that it was the only available material in an electronic format for the author (unfortunately, it is not public).

The original file was in Microsoft Document format. It was opened and saved in a html format. Using Perl scripts, just the headwords were kept, and they were Latinized (in a Setälä-like system) for a phonemic analysis.

Since Erzya harmonic suffixation is considered to be regular and predictable from the phonological form of the stem, dictionaries do not mark the

[5] At least Jack Rueter's (see Rueter (2010), http://giellatekno.uit.no/cgi/d-myv.eng.html) and Timofey Arkhangelskiy's (see Arkhangelskiy (2019), https://bitbucket.org/timarkh/uniparser-grammar-erzya/src/default/) are worth mentioning.

harmonic class of the stem (i.e. which set of allomorphs they are suffixed with). However, verbs always occur in a suffixed form, namely in the infinitive, which offers at least a restricted possibility to look for antiharmonic stems.

3.1 Erzya infinitive forms

Erzya infinitive forms have three typical endings: /-ɑms/, /-ems/ and /-oms/. However, there are different analyses for the morpheme boundaries in verb forms. According to Mészáros (1998, 33) (and similarly Pall, 1996, 20), in forms ending in /-ɑms/ /ɑ/ is always the part of the stem. There are two types of verbs of which infinitive forms end in /-ems/ or /-oms/. In some stems, /e/ or /o/ belongs to the stem, in others it belongs to the suffix. There are some forms which show whether the vowel is the part of the stem or not: see Table 1.

meaning	'stand, be'	'understand'
INF	/ɑʃtʲe-ms/	/tʃɑrkodʲ-ems/
PST.3S	/ɑʃtʲe-sʲ/	/tʃɑrkodʲ-sʲ/
PST.3P	/ɑʃtʲe-sʲtʲ/	/tʃɑrkodʲ-sʲtʲ/
IMP.2S	/ɑʃtʲe-k/	/tʃɑrkodʲ-tʲ/

1. Table: Different morpheme boundaries for similarly looking infinitve forms

However, paradigms in Mészáros (1998, 15–16) show that not even /ɑ/ is present in all verb forms (c. f. /kortɑms/ 'speak:INF' : /korti/ 'speak:PRS.3S'), and it is also true for stems in which /o/ or /e/ are analyzed to be the part of the stem (e. g. /ɑʃtʲems/ 'stand:INF' : /ɑʃtʲi/ 'stand:PRS.3S', moreover /ɑʃtʲɑn/ 'stand:PRS.1S' and /ɑʃtʲɑt/ 'stand:PRS.2S', c. f. /kortɑn/ 'speak:PRS.1S' and /kortɑt/ 'speak:PRS.2S').

Bartens (1999, 122) states that there are stems with stem-final /ɑ/, and this vowel-final stem is used in all the forms of the verb. On the contrary, all verbs with final /o/ or /e/ also have a consonant-final stem (the identical form but without the /o/ or /e/), which is used in more forms when the final vowel is /e/ (no examples presented). Bartens also adds that verbs with final /o/ or /e/ also have an /ɑ/-final stem, used in the first and second singular of the present tense (see above).

Keresztes (1990, 39) (and similarly Keresztes, 2011, 76) states that all Erzya verbs, despite what kind of vowel the verb stem contains at the end of the vowel-final stem, also have a consonant-final stem. However, he says nothing on the distribution of the two stem forms.

In the examples shown by Серебренников et al. (1993, 19–20), the morpheme boundary is sometimes before, sometimes after /e/ and /o/. Although there is a case in the introduction, in which the morpheme boundary is before /ɑ/ (Серебренников et al. 1993, 17, 599: *сок|амс-иза|мс* 'till the soil'), it must be a typo since the morpheme boundary is at the expected place in the dictionary (Серебренников et al. 1993, 599: *сока|мс* 'plow', *сока|мс-иза|мс* 'till the earth').

The problem of the morpheme boundary can be crucial from the point of view of antiharmony. If we find an infinitive ending in /-ems/ where we expect /-oms/ (or vice versa), but the vowel belongs to the stem, it has nothing to do with antiharmony: at most we have to conclude that the stem is disharmonic. Unfortunately, grammars of Erzya do not help much in this case. They never state that stem types are completely lexicalized or (at least in some cases) they are determined by phonotactics (possible syllable structures). Nonetheless, based on the presented examples, it can be clear that stem types are at least partially lexicalized. Stem-final vowel is present in many cases when it is not neccessary at all from the pont of view of phonotactics: /vɑnoms/ 'watch:INF' : /vɑnosʲ/ 'watch:PRT.3S' (Bartens, 1999, 129), /idʲems/ 'save:INF' : /idʲesʲ/ 'save:PRT.3S' (Цыганкин, 1980, 277) etc. On the contrary, there are cases when epenthesis would be pertinent, however, the consonant-final stem is used: /kɑndoms/ 'carry:INF' : /kɑndsʲtʲ/ 'carry:PRT.3P' (Keresztes, 1990, 41), /tʲerʲdʲems/ 'call:INF' : /tʲerʲdʲsʲtʲ/ 'call:PRT.3P', /mɑksoms/ 'give:INF' : /mɑkst/ 'give:IMP:2S' (Цыганкин, 1980, 277) etc. However, it still cannot be excluded that phonotactics can play some role at least in some cases. For example, Фейеш (2005) argues that although the epenthesis of /i/ in Komi-Zyryan verb forms depends on syllable structure in most of the cases, some borderline cases can be lexicalized, and other factors (e. g. the inner morphological structure of the stem) can also play some role.

3.2 Method and results

To find antiharmonic stems, we should check whether there are stems in which the last vowel before /-ems/ is back and the consonant immediately preceding it is not palatalized; or /-oms/ is preceded by a front vowel or a stem-final palatalized consonant. However, even in these cases we have to check whether the /e/ or /o/ belongs to the suffix: if not, it does not say anything about the antiharmonicity of the stem; if yes, it is a clear sign of antiharmonicity. However, we cannot be sure that the stem will behave in an antiharmonic way with all the suffixes. However, the opposite is also true: if the infinitive shows a harmonic way of suffixation, it does not exclude that the stem is suffixed by the unexpected allomorph in some cases. Despite these restrictions, the method gives us possibility to find at least some antiharmonic stems, if they exist.

Based on these considerations, all the headwords ending in /oms/, /ems/ or /ɑms/ were collected from Mészáros and Sirmankine (2003) and they were counted according to the consonant before these endings by another Perl script.[6] The results are presented in Table 2.

Consonant	/e/	/o/	/ɑ/
Non-palatalized dental	18	713	216
Palatalized dental or /j/	778	0	357
Labial	102	153	108
Velar	19	19	50
Alveolar	10	6	47

2. Table: Infinitive endings with different stem final consonants

It is striking that palatalized dentals and /j/ are never followed by /-oms/. Moreover, non-palatalized dentals are overwhelmingly followed by /-oms/, and only exclusively by /-ems/. Although in all these cases the last vowel of the stem is /i/ or /e/, it seems that it is strongly predictable whether an infinitive ends in /-oms/ or /-ems/ just based on whether the consonant before it is palatalized or not. Most of the exceptions (where the last vowel is front but the consonant before /-ems/ is non-palatalized dental) can be devided into two groups:

- onomatopoetic words: /biznems/ 'to bumble'[7], /viʒnems/ 'to buzz, to whiz etc.', /dirnems/ 'to rattle, to crackle' ($\sim$ /dʲirnʲems/ 'to bumble, to bluster, to crackle'), /zeznems/ 'to grizzle, to weep, to snivel; to moan, to grumble; to murmur, to mutter', /irnems/ 'to burr, to bellow', /kiʒnems/ 'to rattle (human, animal)', /kirnems/ 'to snore, to rattle'[8], /kitnems/ 'to giggle, to snicker', /rʲiknems/ 'to blub, to sob, to weep', /tiʒn-ems/ 'to fizzle, to sizzle, to huss';[9]
- ending in a sibilant or a cluster containing a sibilant: /pezems/ 'to wash (head)', /pivsems/ 'to thresh out, to thrash out', /rʲez-ems/ 'to atrophy, to waste', /rʲiznems/ 'to grieve, to sorrow'.

On the one hand, onomatopoetic words tend to behave exceptionally in phonology cross-linguistically (c.f. Fudge 1970). On the other hand, as it has been shown above, dental sibilants tend to behave somewhat exceptionally in harmony: they do not undergo harmony in suffixes. The two phenomena seem to be related. The only case which cannot be categorized into either group is /piʒeldems/ 'to be green', which will be discussed below.

In the case of labials and velars, the situation is also simple. When the last vowel of the stem is front, the infinitive ends in /-ems/, when the last vowel is back, the infinitive ends in /-oms/. However, alveolars show a somewhat different picture. Most of the endings after alveolars with a last (and only) back vowel are /oms/: /vɑt͡ʃoms/ 'to get/be hungry', /kut͡ʃoms/ 'to send', /pɑnʒoms/ 'to open', /puʒoms/ 'to lose plant, to get dead (about flowers), to parch', /ut͡ʃoms/ 'to wait', /t͡ʃɑt͡ʃoms/ 'to be born'. However, there are four similar forms ending in /ems/: /lɑnt͡ʃems/ 'to squat, to hunker', /mɑnt͡ʃems/ 'to fool, to cheat etc.', /tokʃems/ 'to touch, to poke', /jɑvʃems/ 'to divide, to apportion, to distribute, to share out etc.'.

It seems that in all the last cases /e/ can belong to the stem. The vocabulary in Pall (1996), which contains information on whether the third person singular ending of the past tense form is attached to the vowel-final or to the consonant-final stem, contains only /mɑnt͡ʃems/ 'to fool, to cheat etc.'. A Google search on the Internet gives forms like *ланчес(т)ь* 's/he hunkers (they hunker)', *манчес(т)ь* 's/he fools (they fool)', *токшес(т)ь* 's/he touches (they touch)', *явшес(т)ь* 's/he shares out (they share out)'. On the contrary, forms like **ланчс(т)ь* 's/he hunkers (they hunker)', **манчс(т)ь* 's/he fools (they fool)', **токшс(т)ь* 's/he touches (they

[6] NB! These are not always stem-final consonants, since the vowel before /ms/ may belong to the stem; in the case of /ɑ/, according to some grammars cited above, it always belongs to the stem.

[7] C. f. /biznʲems/ 'to go sour, to ferment (about milk)'.

[8] C. f. /kirnʲems/ 'to contract, to shorten etc.'.

[9] One of my reviewers criticizes me for not distinguishing front [i] and centralized [ï]; they also state that in some cases the latter one occurs as a phoneme (not as an allophone of /i/ after non-palatalized dentals), even in some of the examples above. However, since centralization of front vowels, phonemic or allophonic, does not seem to affect harmony, I do not see the relevance of these facts here.

touch)', **явис(т)ь* 's/he shares out (they share out) etc.' are not attested. Nonetheless, it is easy to notice that in all these forms we would find such consonant clusters which are quite unusual even for Erzya. Moreover, if it was a case of inner disharmony in a stem, we would expect that it occurs more times and in more random phonological environments. Consequently, we cannot exclude that /e/ is epenthetic in these forms. If it is, then the stem must be antiharmonic. However, since we have no clear evidence for that, the question must be kept open.

It seems to be easy to find a phonetically based explanation for this ambiguous behaviour of alveolars. Alveolars are articulated near the palate, therefore they are near the palatal(ized) consonants. This could be a reason for them to behave as palatalized dentals in certain cases. However, it contradicts the claim by Имайкина (1996, 9) that alveolars are always "hard" (see Footnote 2.2).

3.3 Some other observations

The statistics presented in Table 2 show an unexpected tendency. As we have mentioned before, according to the literature, when the infinitive ends in /ɑms/, /ɑ/ always belongs to the stem. This suggests that it has nothing to do with (morpho)phonology. However, statistics show that after harmonic consonants (dentals) harmonic vowels (/o/ and /e/) are much more frequent (more than two and a half times) then neutral (non-alternating) /ɑ/. In the case of labials, harmonic vowels also prevail (it is less striking since numbers are divided between /o/ and /e/), although the range is a bit lower. However, in the other cases /ɑ/ prevails: slightly in the case of velars and drastically in the case of alveolars (although the number of examples is almost negligible if we compare it to the number of cases with dentals). The question emerges, whether the choice between /ɑ/ on the one side and /o/ or /e/ on the other side can be somehow conditioned. It may be worth comparing those cases when forms differ only in the vowel before /ms/.

As for /-ɑms/ vs. /-oms/, in two cases the two stem types are opposed: /kot͡ʃkɑms/ 'to choose, to pick etc.' vs. /kot͡ʃkoms/ 'to stub, to weed out', /pɑlɑms/ 'to kiss' vs. /pɑloms/ 'to burn (up/down/away)' and in one case we have alternation: /t͡sʲokordɑms/ ~ /t͡sʲokordoms/ 'to sing (about nightingale)'.

In the case of /-ɑms/ vs. /-ems/, there is only one opposition: /puvorʲɑms/ 'to turn, to rotate, to curl, to spin' vs. /puvorʲems/ 'to crust (over), to get knobby etc.'. Alternation is much more general: /ilʲtʲɑms/ ~ /ilʲtʲems/ 'to escort, to see off/out', /kemelʲdʲɑms/ ~ /kemelʲdʲems/ 'to sew ornaments etc.', /kengelʲɑms/ ~ /kengelʲems/ 'to lie', /ket͡ʃkerʲɑms/ ~ /ket͡ʃkerʲems/ 'to butt, to hurn, to stab etc.', /mendʲɑms/ ~ /mendʲems/ 'to bent, to bow, to crook etc.', /menstʲɑms/ ~ /menstʲems/ 'to make/set free, to rescue', /pupordʲɑms/ ~ /pupordʲems/ 'to bump, to falter, to stumble', /rʲeʒnʲɑms/ ~ /rʲeʒnʲems/ 'to go sour, to ferment (about milk)', /sɑnʲdʲɑms/ ~ /sɑnʲdʲems/ 'to grub up, to exterminate', /tolkɑnʲtʲɑ-ms/ ~ /tolkɑnʲtʲems/ 'to make oneself sweaty, to languish, to fatigue', /t͡ʃemerʲdʲɑms/ ~ /t͡ʃemerʲdʲems/ 'to press, to squeeze', /t͡ʃirʲtʲɑms/ ~ /t͡ʃirʲtʲems/ 'to twist, to warp etc.', /ezʲelʲdʲɑms/ ~ /ezʲelʲdʲems/ 'to lie'.

There is only one stem with an infinitive ending in /-oms/ and /-ems/: /piʒeldoms/ ~ /piʒeldems/ 'to be (vividly) green'. Since the last vowel of the stem, /piʒeldems/ is front, we would expect here the /-ems/ ending. Moreover, since the verb is derived from the adjective /piʒe/ 'green', we could also aspect a palatalized form of the derivational suffix, something like */piʒelʲdʲ(-ems)/. However, although there are verbs ending in /lʲdʲ(-ems)/, there are no verbs derived from an adjective (or other word) with the suffix /-lʲdʲ-/.

On the contrary, there are some other verbs with the meaning 'to be coloured a certain colour' derived from the adjective meaning the colour by the suffix /ld/: /ɑʃoldoms/ 'to be (vividly) white' (← /ɑʃo/ 'white'), /oʒoldoms/ 'to be (vividly) yellow' (← /oʒo/ 'yellow'), /rɑuʒoldoms/ 'to be black' (← /rɑuʒo/ 'black'). In all these cases the basis of the stem contains back vowels.[10]

There are also some other, semantically farther derivations, all with back vowels: /nuzʲɑldoms/ 'to be lazy, to laze, to idle' (←?, ~? /nuzʲɑks/ 'lazy'), /kɑvtoldoms/ 'to doubt, to hesitate, to vacillate' (← /kɑvto/ 'two')[11], /gumboldoms/ ~ /kumboldoms/ 'to play in all colours of the rainbow' (←? /kumbo/ ~ /kumbɑ/ 'carpet'). The last case, in all probability, is not a dervation, but speakers may feel a connection between colourful carpets and other things playing in all colours of the rainbow.

[10]There are some colour names with front vowels, but verbs meaning 'being those colours' are derived in a different way: (/senʲ/ 'blue' → /senʲeʒdʲ(ems)/ 'to be (vividly) blue', /jɑksʲtʲerʲe/ 'red' → /jɑksʲtʲerʲdʲ(ems)/ 'to be (vividly) red'

[11]C. f. Hungarian *két* 'two', *kételkedik* 'to doubt'.

The alternation /piʒeldoms/ ~ /piʒeldems/ can be explained as follows. Since the vowels in the stem are front, the front allomorphs of the harmonic suffixes should be attached. However, stems ending in non-palatalized dentals are typically suffixed with back allomorphs of the harmonic suffixes. These can take an analogical effect, which can be strengthened by the fact that all morphosemantically analogical derived verbs are suffixed with the back allomorphs. The harmonic pattern and the lexico-semantical patterns are in conflict in this case, which results in vacillation. Moreover, in this case an Internet search shows that the vowel before /ms/ belongs to the suffix, not the stem: *пижелдсь*, **пижелдэсь*, **пижелдось* 'be.green:PST.3S'; *пижелдсть*, **пижелдость*, **пижелдэсть* 'be.green:PST.3P'; *пижелдт*, **пижелдэк*, **пижелдок* 'be.green:IMP.2S'.

There is another similar case: /mazildoms/ 'to be beautiful' (← /mazi(j)/ 'beautiful'). In this case, the dictionary (Mészáros and Sirmankine, 2003) does not contain the infinitive form with the front allomorph (/mazildems/). One should argue the reason in this case is that the last vowel is neutral or that it stands after a non-palatal dental, therefore, it is somewhat retracted.[12] This retractedness can weaken the triggering of the front allomorph, and it can be a reason that there is no vacillation, but the back allomorphs of harmonic suffixes are used in all cases. Notwithstanding, an online search shows that the form /mazildems/ exists in the Erzya part of the MarlaMuter dictionary (https://marlamuter.org/muter/Эрзя/) (but the same source does not know the form /mazildoms/). The same source states that the vowel does not belong to the stem, and the Internet search can prove it: *мазылдсь*, **мазылдэсь*, **мазылдось* 'be.beautiful:PST.3S' – however, other forms (PST.3P, IMP) are not attested and Pall (1996) does not contain this verb either.

Apart from /piʒeld-/ and /mazild-/, there were no stems found in which the last vowel is front but the stem-final consonant is non-palatalized. Since other forms show that in these verbs the last vowel of the infinive belongs to the suffix, forms with back allomorphs of harmonic suffixes must be considered antiharmonic, although the stems are not unequivocally antiharmonic, since both can also be suffixed by the front allomorphs. We can conclude that these stems are alternetively antiharmonic.

Stems /lɑnt͡ʃ(e?)-/ 'to squat, to hunker', /mɑnt͡ʃ(e?)-/ 'to fool, to cheat etc.', /tokʃ(e-)/ 'to touch, to poke', /jɑvʃ(e-)/ 'to divide, to apportion, to distribute, to share out etc.' can be considered antiharmonic if we can raise the possibility that the /e/ in them does not belong to the stem.

Based on the verbs, we have a clue what kind of stems we have to look for among other parts of speech if we want to find antiharmonic ones. These are the stems in which the last vowel is front, but the stem-final consonant is non-palatized and stems in which the last vowel is back and the stem-final consonant is alveolar.

4 Testing dubious stems

Having determined what kind of stems can be antiharmonic by a higher probability, first we have to collect them. Again, another Perl script was used on the same material. The number of headwords with a front last vowel and a stem-final non-palatalized dental consonant is somewhat over 450, the number of headwords with a back last vowel and a stem-final alveolar consonant is over 60. However, not all of these are suffixable stems (moreover, adjectives and numerals are suffixed rarely).

Since dictionaries do not provide information on the suffixation of these stems (except for the occasionally occuring sample sentences, in a fragment of which the stem is suffixed with a harmonizing suffix), we have to test the existence of the forms by a search on the Internet. Considering the facts that Erzya material on the Internet is quite restricted;[13] some of the tested words are rare; suffixed forms are usually rarer than unsuffixed ones and not all the suffixes are harmonic , and – because of lack of time and resources – not all the possible forms showing (anti)harmony can be tested, it is expectable that we will not find enough material in all the cases. However, the following forms were tested:

- form with the ablative suffix -/do/ : -/to/ : -/de/ : -/te/ : -/d^{j}e/ : -/t^{j}e/;
- form with the inessive suffix -/so/ : -/se/;
- form with the elative suffix -/sto/ : -/ste/;
- form with the abessive suffix -/tomo/ : -/teme/ : -/t^{j}eme/;[14]

[12]In Mordvinic languages, similarly to Russian /i/, front vowels following non-palatalazed consonants having a palatalized counterpart are somewhat retracted.

[13]Moreover, since material on other languages is much more, sometimes they produce irrelevant search results which mask the necessary information.

[14]The abessive case also has suffix allomorphs -/vtomo/ : -/vt^{j}eme/, which are used after a stem-final vowel.

- forms with the 3S possessive suffixes: -/ozo/ : -/eze/ (for singular) and -/onzo/ : -/enze/ (for plural).[15]

Unfortunately, local suffixes are rarely used with stems meaning humans, and that fact makes testing even more difficult.

4.1 Stems with a stem-final alveolar

Since if the last vowel in the infinitive form is analyzed as the part of the suffix, two of our possibly antiharmonic verb stems /lɑnt͡ʃ-/ 'to squat, to hunker' and /mɑnt͡ʃ-/ 'to fool, to cheat etc.' end in the cluster /nt͡ʃ/, it would be worth starting the test with nominals ending in the same cluster. However, we found no such nominal stems. The case with /jɑvʃ-/ 'to divide, to apportion, to distribute, to share out etc.' is similar. However, the fourth verb stem, /tokʃ-/ 'to touch, to poke' ends in a cluster /kʃ/, which is quite frequent among the stems ending in an alveolar. None of these words were found to be systematically suffixed with front allomorphes. The only form with a stem-final /kʃ/ and a front suffix allomorph was /pokʃ-te/ along with several instances of /pokʃ-to/ 'big-ABL'. However, based on this example , it is questionable whether any similarity of alveolars to palatalized consonats plays any role in similar cases: after a palatalized consonant we would expect the -/tʲe/ allomorph of the suffix, -/te/ occurs after stems ending non-palatalized stem final consonants and with a front last vowel.

Moreover, some other forms were also found with a stem-final alveolar consonant and an antiharmonic suffix: /urʲaʒ-enze/ besides several /urʲaʒ-onzo/ 'brother's.wife-PL.3S'; /etaʒ-se/ besides several /etaʒ-so/ 'floor-INE'; /oʃ-se/ besides several /oʃ-so/ 'town-INE'[16] However, it seems that antiharmonic suffixation is very periferic and it is not clear whether it has any connection with the alveolar stem-final consonant.

4.2 Stems with a stem-final non-palatalized dental

Due to the high number of stems with a front last vowel and a stem-final non-palatalized dental consonant, we could not test all the possible stem-suffix combinatons. However, we tried to test at least the more frequent ones of the most typical groups.

One of the most important groups is that of Russian words used in Erzya texts. Antiharmonic forms seem to occur sporadically: /koncʲert-sto/ besides several /koncʲert-ste/ 'concert-ELA'; /alfavit-sto/ besides an /alfavit-ste/ 'alphabet-ELA';[17] /dokument-onzo/ besides several /dokument-enze/ 'document-PL.3S'; /dokument-so/ besides several /dokument-se/ 'document-INE'; /internet-so/ besides several /internet-se/ 'Internet-INE'; /pitʲer-so/ (even twice) besides several /pitʲer-se/ 'Sankt-Petersburg-INE' etc.

We can find similar cases with native Erzya words as well: /velʲks-so/ besides several /velʲks-se/ 'top-INE, above; (sour.)cream-INE'; /lʲezks-ozo/ besides several /lʲezks-eze/ 'help-3S'; /pelʲks-ozo/ besides several /pelʲks-eze/ 'part-3S'; /pelʲks-so/ besides several /pelʲks-se/ 'part-INE'; /tʲeʃks-ozo/ besides several /tʲeʃks-eze/ 'mark-3S'; /tʲeʃks-so/ besides several /tʲeʃks-se/ 'mark-INE' etc.

These forms are very rare and must be considered exceptional. It is worth noticing that some of the examples are from newspapers from the first half of the 20th century. Therefore, this phenomenon cannot be related to language loss. Мосин (2015, 24) shows some other examples when we find /o/ instead of Modern Standard Erzya /e/ after non-palatalized dentals in the newspapers of the twenties and thirties. According to him, these cases reflect different dialectal forms from the time when the linguistic norms were not settled. It is possible that antiharmonic forms even today reflect dialectal forms. Nonetheless, this means that at least in dialects these antiharmonic forms are possible. The only problem can be if all these forms are reflections of dialects in which – similarly to Moksha – we find a reduced vowel (schwa) instead of /o/ and /e/. In this case, we have only an allophonic alternation. Since Moksha orthography uses *o* for the back allomorph of

[15]According to (Keresztes, 1990, 58) or (Bartens, 1999, 72), in these cases the first vowel belongs to the stem. However, it seems that this kind of segmentation is based on language history, and no synchronic facts support this kind of analysis. Since the given vowel is not predictable from the phonological construction of the stem (and not a lexicalized property either), it should be rather analyzed as epenthetic or belonging to the suffix.

[16]This case is debatable because in an earlier version of the text containing the form /oʃ-se/ we find /saranskoj-se/ 'in Saransk' here, and it was changed to /saransk oʃ-se/ 'in the town of Saransk'. It can be a simple typo emerged during the redaction.

[17]However, /alfavit-osʲ/ instead of /alfavit-esʲ/ 'alphabet-DEF.NOM' on the same site. Surprisingly, on the same site we also find the sentence *Те алфавитось теевсь 1862 иестэ ды формовсь 1874 иесто* 'This alphabet was constructed in year 1862 and got its final form in year 1874', in which we find both /ije-sto/ and /ije-ste/ 'year-ELA'. In these case, the use of the back allomorph cannot be explained either by the vowels or the consonants of the stem.

schwa, occuring always after non-palatalized dentals, it is impossible to differentiate whether the reflected dialectal form contains /o/ or /e/.

5 Conclusion

We could identify two verbs, /piʒeld-/ 'to be green' and /mazild-/ 'to be beautiful', which can be suffixed in an antiharmonic way (but harmonic suffixation is also possible). This phenomenon can be explained by the fact that stems with a final non-palatalized dental usually contain back vowels and take back allomorphs of harmonizing suffixes (and it is particularly true for verbs with a deajectival derivational suffix /-ld-/) and they take analogical impact on the suffixation of these stems.

Another group of verbs, /lɑntʃ(e)-/ 'to squat, to hunker', /mɑntʃ(e)-/ 'to fool, to cheat etc.', /tokʃ(e)-/ 'to touch, to poke', /jɑvʃ(e)-/ 'to share out etc.' can be considered antiharmonic or (stem-internally) disharmonic depending on the morphological analysis. In this case, supposed antiharmony can be explained by the resemblence of alveolars to palatalized dentals (proximity of place of articulation). If these cases are treated as antiharmonic ones, these stems are the only consistently antiharmonic stems known.

We could not find any antiharmonic stems among nominals, but we found that stems with a last front vowel and a stem-final non-palatalized dental and stems with a last back vowel and a stem-final alveolar are suffixed in an antiharmonic way at least marginally. However, since no other kind of stems were tested, we cannot state that the degree this kind of antiharmonic behavior is higher than among stems with other kind of phonological structure (c. f. Footnote 17).

In any case, it must be emphasized that this research offers just a basic introspection to the problem of antiharmony in Erzya. A further study of the dialectal background is required and experiments should be made on the degree of acceptability of such forms.

In addition, although only in a marginal case, the results has relevance for the development of Erzya morphological analyzers. For example, it seems that the Giellatekno analyzer is based on the assumption that harmony is complitely regular in Erzya. The analysis of the forms *пижелдэмс, пижелдомс, мазылдэмс* and *мазылдомс* suggests that the infinitive suffix is simpy cut of and the harmonic class is generated based on the phonological structure of the stem. Therefore, although the the *мазылд*-stem is generated based on the form *мазылдомс*, the analyzer does not recognize it. On the contrary, it can analyze the form *мазылдэмс*, but it is analyzed as a form of *мазылдомс*. Since its dictionary contains both *пижелдэмс* and *пижелдомс*, the form *пижелдэмс* is analyzed once as a form of *пижелдэмс*, once as a form of *пижелдомс*, but the form *пижелдомс* remains unanalyzed. These wierd results could be avoided if the determination of the harmonic class of the stem was based on the form of the infinitive suffix. However, it must be emphasized, that this anomaly exhibits only with these two (four?) verbs.

Acknowledgments

The research was financed by the NKFI 119863 Experimental and theoretical investigation of vowel harmony patterns. I would like to thank Péter Rebrus. I am particularly grateful for the assistance given by Nóra Wenszky and for Boglárka Janurik for the consultation on Erzya data. I am obliged to the reviewers for drawing my attention to certain important facts I left out of account. My special thanks are extended to György Soros for his help of founding the Department of Theoretical Linguistics of the Eötvös Loránd University.

References

Timofey Arkhangelskiy. 2019. Corpora of social media in minority uralic languages. In *Proceedings of the fifth Workshop on Computational Linguistics for Uralic Languages, Tartu, Estonia, January 7 - January 8, 2019*, page 125–140. Association for Computational Linguistics.

Raija Bartens. 1999. *Mordvalaiskielten rakenne ja kehitys*. Suomalais-Ugrilainen Seura, Helsinki.

Erik Fudge. 1970. Phonological structure and 'expressiveness'. *Journal of Linguistics*, 6(2):161–188.

Auli Hakulinen, Maria Vilkuna, Riitta Korhonen, Vesa Koivisto, Tarja Riitta Heinonen, and Irja Alho. 2004. *Iso suomen kielioppi*. Suomalaisen Kirjallisuuden Seura, Hämeenlinna.

László Keresztes. 1990. *Chrestomathia morduinica*. Tankönyvkiadó, Budapest.

László Keresztes. 2011. *Bevezetés a mordvin nyelvészetbe*. Debreceni Egyetemi Kiadó, Debrecen.

Adam Kilgarriff. 2007. Googleology is bad science. *Computational Linguistics*, 33(1):147–151.

Edit Mészáros. 1998. *Erza-mordvin nyelvkönyv kezdőknek és haladóknak*. JATEPress, Szeged.

Edit Mészáros and Raisza Sirmankine. 2003. *Erza-mordvin–magyar szótár*. Savaria University Press, Szombathely.

Valdek Pall. 1996. *Ersa keel. Õpiku konspekt ja sõnaloend*. [Valdek Pall], Tallinn.

Jack Rueter. 2010. *Adnominal person in the morphological system of Erzya*. Suomalais-Ugrilainen Seura, Helsinki.

Л. В. Бондарко and О. Е. Полякова. 1993. *Современные мордовские языки. Фонетика*. Мордовское книжное издательство, Саранск.

М. Д. Имайкина. 1996. *Эрзянский язык. Учебное пособие для русскоязычных студентов. В 2 частях*. Издательство Мордовского Унивеситета, Саранск.

М. В. Мосин. 2015. Отражение гласных и согласных фонем в текстах эрзянских газет 1920–1938 гг. *Финно-угорский мир*, 23(2):22–30.

Б. А. Серебренников, Р. Н. Бузакова, and М. В. Мосин. 1993. *Эрзянь–рузонь валкс*. <Русский язык>, Москва.

Ласло Фейеш. 2005. Эпентетическое *ы* в глагольных формах коми языка. In *История, современное состояние, перспективы развития языков и культур финно-угорских народов. Материалы III научной конференции финно-угроведов (1-4 июля 2004. г. Сыктывкар)*, pages 215–218. Инстутут языка, литературы и истории Коми науучного центра УрО РАН.

Д. В Цыганкин, editor. 1980. *Грамматика мордовских языков. фонетика, графика, орфография, морфология*. Мордовский государственный университет имени Н. П. Огарева, Саранск.

apPILcation: an Android-based Tool for Learning Mansi

Gábor Bobály[1], **Csilla Horváth**[2,3], **Veronika Vincze**[4]
[1]IT Services Hungary
[2]Research Institute for Linguistics, Hungarian Academy of Sciences
[3]University of Helsinki
[4]MTA-SZTE Research Group on Artificial Intelligence
bobalygabor@gmail.com, naj.agi@gmail.com, vinczev@inf.u-szeged.hu

Abstract

Here we introduce our Android application for Mansi language learning, called apPILcation / PILozhenie / apPILkáció. Learners can select Hungarian, English or Russian as the source language while learning Mansi. Currently, the application offers a general vocabulary practising session as well as a thematic word guessing game. apPILcation is primarily supposed to be used by learners of the Mansi language but language teachers and linguists may also be interested in it. The application can be freely used for anyone interested, and will be soon made available for download.

A cikkben bemutatjuk az apPILkáció / apPILcation / PILozhenie nevű Android-alkalmazásunkat, mely a manysi nyelv elsajátítását, konkrétabban manysi szavak tanítását célozza. Az alkalmazás nyelve választhatóan magyar, orosz vagy angol. Moduljai között találunk általános szókincsre épülő, véletlenszerűen kiválasztott manysi szavakat tanító modult, illetve meghatározott szemantikai mezőhöz (pl. állatok) tartozó szavakra épülő szókitaláló modult. Az alkalmazás elsődlegesen a manysi nyelvtanulók érdeklődésére tarthat számot, de hasznos lehet nyelvészeknek vagy nyelvtanároknak is. Az alkalmazást mindenki számára ingyenesen elérhetővé tesszük.

1 Introduction

Nowadays, the widespread use of the internet and digital technologies offers a variety of possibilities for real-time communication among people around the world. Such interaction is further supported by several language technology tools such as speech to text systems, spellcheckers and machine translation systems, just to name a few. However, minority languages often lack these tools, which might lead to the loss of such languages in the digital space. On the other hand, there are some efforts to revitalize endangered languages, which aim at constructing tools and resources for such languages to be used in digital communication.

In this paper, we focus on Mansi, an endangered language spoken in Western Siberia. Although the number of Mansi native speakers decreases, the prestige of language proficiency and language use is rising, also there is a growing interest towards language acquisition and heritage language acquisition, with special focus on urban learners of Mansi. In order to help such efforts, we implemented apPILcation, an Android application for Mansi language acquisition, freely available for anyone. In this paper, we present the application and its main functionalities. As far as we know, ours is the first attempt to offer an online tool for smartphones for Mansi language learning.

The paper is structured as follows. First we give an overview of some language teaching mobile applications, then we briefly discuss the current sociolinguistic background of the speakers and learners of Mansi. Next, apPILcation is presented in detail, together with its main functionalities. The paper ends with listing some of the possible uses of the application.

2 Background

Mobile-assisted language learning (MALL) has been an emerging field in language teaching recently due to the widespread usage of smartphones in all over the world (Chinnery, 2006). Traxler (2005) defines mobile learning as "Any educational delivery where the sole or prevailing technologies are handheld or palmtop devices". MALL enables

Proceedings of the 6th International Workshop on Computational Linguistics of Uralic Languages, pages 48–55
Wien, Austria, January 10 — 11, 2020.
https://doi.org/10.18653/v1/FIXME

language learners to study whenever and wherever they are, without the need for desktop computers (Miangah and Nezarat, 2012). However, most surveys on MALL investigated only the institutional use of mobile-based learning while only a few analysed their use outside the classroom (Godwin-Jones, 2017). For instance, Stockwell and Hubbard (2013) define ten principles for MALL, e.g. accommodating language learner differences and keeping activities short.

There are several smartphone applications for language learners from bilingual dictionaries to tools offering grammar exercises. However, the number of languages these tools offer courses for is rather limited: solutions are mostly available for widely spoken languages. Just to name a few such applications, Babbel[1], Duolingo[2], Memrise[3] and Busuu[4] are among the most well-known applications for language learning. Table 1 shows the languages with available courses in the above applications (as of November 2019). Data on the number of the native speakers for each language come from the English Wikipedia.

As can be seen, it is primarily world languages, in addition, smaller languages mostly spoken in Europe that are taught in these applications, not to mention extinct languages like Latin or constructed and fictional languages (beside Esperanto, Klingon and High Valyrian are also available in Duolingo, the two latter owe their popularity to certain television series).

Concerning the mobile-assisted language learning for minority Uralic languages, we are aware of only few applications, e.g. Laring[5], developed at the University of Tromsø for teaching Southern Saami.[6] The system teaches words belonging to different word groups to the user: it reads out the Southern Saami equivalent of Norwegian words, while in another task, listening comprehension can also be practised – a picture corresponding to the heard Saami word should be chosen. Beside this, we are aware of some user-generated Memrise courses for Uralic and Siberian languages, e.g. Ingrian[7], Livonian[8], Kven[9] and Yakut[10]. Also, there are some courses available that contain only some tens of words for languages such as Ulch[11] and Enets[12]. The Mansi version consists of 11 elements (one of which is translated incorrectly), using an inconsistent spelling. Thus our apPILcation is proved not to be the first MALL application for Mansi, but it has very good chance to incorporate more material and attract more users than its predecessor.

3 Mansi language, its speakers and learners

Mansi is an endangered language spoken in Western Siberia. Mansi plays limited role in its Russian-dominated, multiethnic and multilingual environment, its usage is heavily affected by the loss of the traditional way of life and rapid urbanisation as well. While the Mansi have been (and in some respect still are) regarded as followers of traditional, semi-nomadic lifestyles, and are expected to live in rural conditions, the majority of the Mansi live in a multi-ethnic urban environment.

The principles of Soviet language policy according to which the Mansi literary language and written standard have been designed kept changing from time to time. The first, Latin alphabet for Mansi was created in 1931 at the Institute of the Peoples of the North. It was in use for a short period, in 1937 the Mansi language planners had to switch to Cyrillic transcription. This writing system is in use since then, and underwent only minor changes. The marking of vowel length and special characters absent from the Russian alphabet started to appear in printed materials in the 1980s. Since the 1990s two parallel spellings are in use (differing only in one element), one used by the leading specialists (mainly following the Soviet academic policy, publishing a small amount of Mansi texts) and the journalists (using and promoting the language on a daily basis, with the largest active number of followers). Taking into consideration the history and the status of the Mansi language, in our application we use the colloquial literary written Mansi standard, that is, the

[1]`https://www.babbel.com/`

[2]`https://www.duolingo.com/`

[3]`https://www.memrise.com/`

[4]`https://www.busuu.com/`

[5]`http://divvun.no/laring/laring.html`

[6]When writing this paper, we could have access only to the iPhone version of the application, the Android version being unavailable for download.

[7]`https://decks.memrise.com/course/2107565/ingrian/`

[8]`https://decks.memrise.com/course/5603933/livonian/`

[9]`https://decks.memrise.com/course/5596403/kven/`

[10]`https://decks.memrise.com/course/362501/basic-yakut/`

[11]`https://decks.memrise.com/course/1064732/ulch-language/`

[12]`https://decks.memrise.com/course/1843983/family-words-in-enets/`

Language	Number of native speakers	Babbel	Duolingo	Memrise	Busuu
Chinese	1500M		•	•	•
Spanish	400M	•	•	•	•
English	332M		•		•
Hindi	370M		•		
Arabic	300M		•	•	•
Portuguese	230M	•	•	•	•
French	220M	•	•	•	•
Russian	145M	•	•	•	•
Japanese	126M		•	•	•
German	90M	•	•	•	•
Korean	78M		•	•	
Vietnamese	70M		•		
Italian	63M	•	•	•	•
Turkish	60M	•	•	•	•
Polish	50M	•	•	•	•
Indonesian	43M	•	•		
Ukranian	35M		•		
Romanian	24M		•		
Dutch	22M	•	•	•	
Greek	20M		•		
Hungarian	15M		•		
Czech	12M		•		
Catalan	10M		•		
Swedish	9M	•	•	•	
Hebrew	6M		•		
Danish	5,5M	•	•	•	
Guarani	4,8M		•		
Norwegian	4,6M	•	•	•	
Mongolian	3,6M			•	
Slovenian	2,5M			•	
Swahili	2M		•		
Welsh	610K		•		
Icelandic	310K			•	
Irish	260K		•		
Navajo	170K		•		
Hawaiian	2K		•		
Esperanto	0		•		
Klingon	0		•		
Latin	0		•		
High Valyrian	0		•		

Table 1: Languages with language courses available on smartphones.

Cyrillic-based form of spelling used in the press.

Although the prestige of Mansi language and culture is rising, the number of Mansi speakers is critically low. The Mansi speakers' community is traditionally divided into three major age groups (cf. Skribnik and Koshkaryova (2006)). The eldest speakers were born and raised in monolingual Mansi families and remained more or less monolingual Mansi themselves, with only a limited command of Russian. The middle-aged speakers were born and raised in monolingual Mansi families and speak Mansi as their mother tongue, in line with becoming Mansi-Russian bilinguals through education, and generally they live in Russian-dominated multilingual environment. The youngest generation of Mansi speakers consists of considerably less people than the former two, and with the exception of those being raised in a few peripherical Mansi villages to be found outside the Khanty-Mansi Autonomous Okrug, none of them can be considered as Mansi monolingual even until their school years. Thus the level of the speakers' proficiency in Mansi is typically related to their age: the older the speakers are, the more likely they are to have native competence in Mansi. This general tendency is often counterbalanced by the speaker's place of birth and residence: younger speakers born and raised in smaller, monolingual Mansi settlements often have good command of the Mansi language.

The majority of Mansi children are born outside the Mansi-speaking settlements. They usually reside in multiethnic, multicultural towns and cities, and live in families with Russian as the language of communication. Their Mansi parents usually have not taught them the Mansi language, hence these children cannot acquire it while listening to their parents' conversations either (since the parents tend to use Russian between themselves, as well), which leaves education as the only possible domain available of Mansi language acquisition for children. A small number of alternative institutions were founded in larger, urbanised settlements with a large Mansi population to complement Mansi children's knowledge of their heritage, culture and language, which they could not completely acquire within their family, but they do not serve as stable domains for language use either (cf. Horváth (2015, 2016)).

The group of middle-aged and especially young language learners, who had no ties with Mansi-speaking families or other domains, or for some reason were unable to acquire the Mansi language in their family, but who are still interested and motivated to attend Mansi language courses at school or to study the language on their own, form our main target group.

4 apPILcation / PILozhenie

Our Android-based tool is called apPILcation in English, apPILkáció in Hungarian and PILozhenie in Russian, *pil* meaning "berry" in Mansi. Our idea behind the name was that by using the application, it is as easy to pick up words in Mansi as picking up berries in the forest.

4.1 The Underlying Dictionary

Researchers of the Mansi language already compiled some dictionaries of the language about one hundred years ago, which were only lately published (Munkácsi and Kálmán, 1986; Kannisto, 2013). These dictionaries contain words from all the dialects, also from those that are now extinct. There are also some modern dictionaries of the Northern Mansi dialect available (Rombandeeva, 2005; Rombandeeva and Kuzakova, 1982). These dictionaries form the base for the vocabulary used in our application, all of which come from the Northern dialect of Mansi.

The vocabulary used in the application is built on an online Mansi dictionary that contains approximately 20,000 entries (Horváth et al., 2017). The Mansi forms were retrieved from the PDF versions of Rombandeeva's and Kuzakova's, as well as Rombandeeva's dictionaries (Rombandeeva, 2005; Rombandeeva and Kuzakova, 1982) by means of optical character recognition, then lexical entries from different sources were merged. The Mansi lexemes are supplemented with the Russian translation given by the dictionaries, and Hungarian and English translations were provided by linguists. Thus, the potential learners of Mansi can choose whether they want to learn Mansi with Russian, English or Hungarian as the source language.

Table 2 contains the number of vocabulary items for each language in the dictionary.

4.2 Functionalities

The main functionalities of the application are as follows. First, a randomized Mansi word is shown to the learner, together with its translation in the given source language, so that he or she can check whether he or she already knows the word. If not, he or she

Language	Entry
Mansi	13,948
Russian	14,344
Hungarian	2,334
English	458

Table 2: Statistics on languages.

can now memorize the word. Second, there is a possibility for playing some quizzes, for instance, the learner can choose certain topics (e.g. colors, family terms, berries or animals) and he or she has to match Mansi words that belong to these semantic categories with their other language equivalents. In this way, words with similar meaning can be learnt and practised together. Third, some information on Mansi grammar, Mansi geography and Mansi culture is also available in the application, in order to deepen cultural knowledge on Mansi as well.

4.2.1 Vocabulary Learning

First, the user can select which language pair s/he wants to work with: Mansi–Hungarian, Mansi–Russian, Mansi–English, Hungarian–Mansi, Russian–Mansi or English–Mansi (see Figure 1[13]). Next, by tapping the button *Give me a new word* a word is shown to him or her in the selected source language and he or she can decide whether sh/he knows the meaning in the target language. By tapping the button *Show the target language equivalent*, he or she can check the meaning of the word as shown in Figure 2.

4.2.2 Thematic Word-guessing Games

In the case of thematic word-guessing games, the user can select which semantic group of words he or she wants to practice. Then a word is shown to him or her from the given semantic field, together with four words from the target language, out of which one is correct while the other three are incorrect. By clicking on the correct equivalent, it turns green, indicating that it is the correct answer (see Figure 3). On the other hand, incorrect words are highlighted with red when clicking on them (see Figures 4 and 5). By clicking on the button *New quiz*, a new word is offered to the user for practice.

Currently, apPILcation contains four semantic groups, namely, colors, family terms, berries and animals, which we are planning to extend with other

[13]In the screenshots, we use the Hungarian version of the application as this is another Uralic language.

Figure 1: Dictionaries available in apPILcation.

semantic groups of words in the near future.

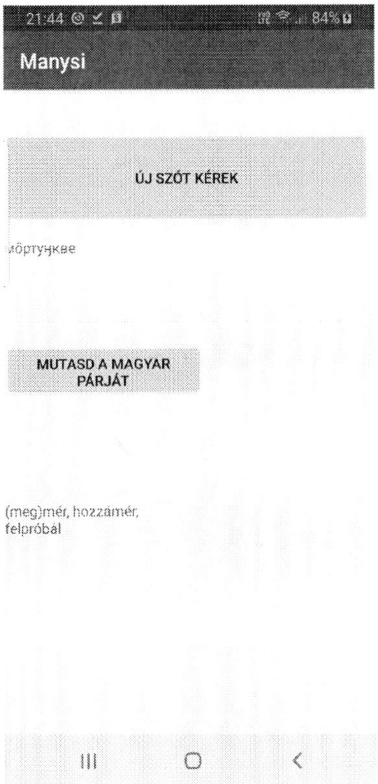

Figure 2: A Mansi–Hungarian entry.

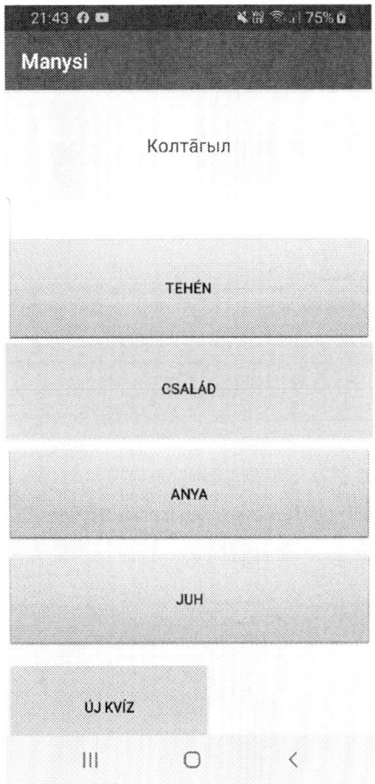

Figure 3: Correct selection of the meaning of the word.

5 Applicability

Our apPILcation may serve various purposes in its present state. It may be used by any user who can read Russian, English or Hungarian, and Mansi written in Cyrillic. We expect attention from the experts and university students specialised on Ob-Ugric languages from all over the world, but first and foremost from pupils, students and Mansi language teachers living on the territory of the Khanty-Mansi Autonomous Okrug.

The word matching module of the application is targeted for beginning language learners, especially for pupils on 1-5 classes. In the beta version of the application, the module contains four word sets, which can be extended according the users' feedback.

The randomised Mansi word learning module is targeted for more advanced language learners, especially for pupils of senior classes and students, who spend regular, but short periods using the applica-

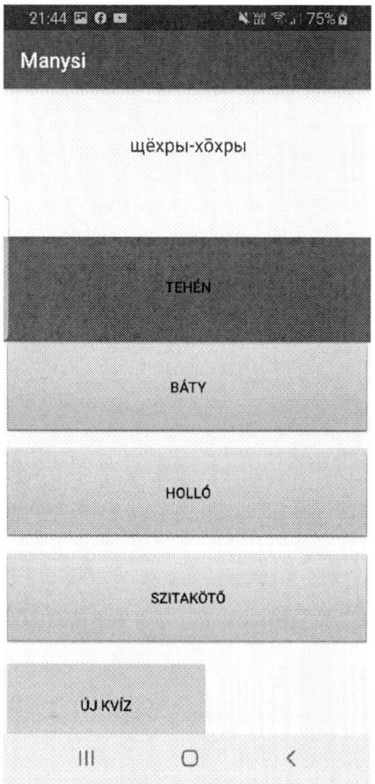

Figure 4: Incorrect selection of the meaning of the word.

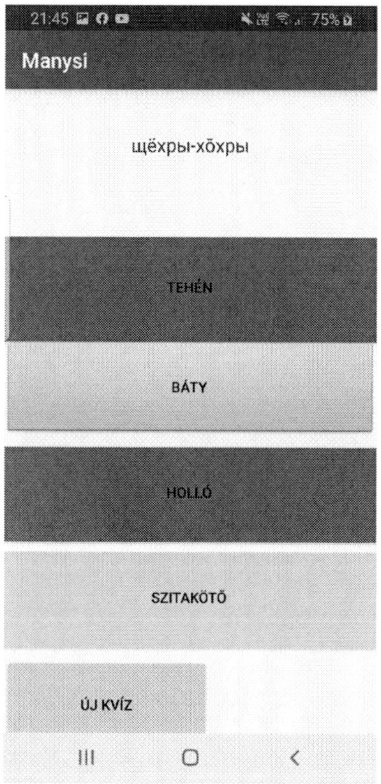

Figure 5: Incorrect, then correct selection of the meaning of the word.

tion.

Both modules are ideal for independent language learning. The word matching module may be used to complement teacher assisted language learning as well.

apPILcation will be open access and it is going to be available for use without charge. The advertisement of the program seems to be unproblematic due to the creators' connection with European specialists possibly interested in the application on the one hand, and both offline and online Mansi speaker groups on the other hand. The promotion is planned to take place on the different pages and in chat threads of the most popular Russian social media site, as well as in reports or advertisements to be published in the only Mansi newspaper and the only Mansi journal for children. Creators expect to get direct feedback via social media pages created on two social media sites, via the email address of the application, while indirect feedback with the help of the Mansi intermediators and distributors of the application, first and foremost from specialists working in press and educational institutions.

6 Conclusions

In this paper, we presented our Android application for Mansi language learning, called apPILcation / PILozhenie / apPILkáció. Learners can select Hungarian, English or Russian as the source language while learning Mansi. Currently, the application offers a general vocabulary practising session as well as a thematic word guessing game for specific groups of words (e.g. colors). apPILcation is primarily supposed to be used by learners of the Mansi language but it may serve useful for language teachers and linguists as well.

The application can be freely used for anyone interested, and will be soon made available for download.

As future work, we would like to extend the vocabulary of apPILcation, besides, we would like to implement other modules for assisting vocabulary learning. Moreover, we would like to add some grammar-based drills and tasks to the modules of the application. Lastly, we would like to create APPLEcation (priLOMTzhenie in Russian and ALMAlkazás in Hungarian), the iPhone version of apPILcation.

Acknowledgements

We would like to thank our anonymous reviewers for their useful comments and remarks. Special thanks are due to Reviewer 2, who raised our attention to the user-generated modules of Memrise.

References

George M. Chinnery. 2006. Going to the MALL: Mobile Assisted Language Learning. *Language Learning & Technology*, 10(1):9–16.

Robert Godwin-Jones. 2017. Smartphones and language learning. *Language Learning & Technology*, 21(2):3–17.

Csilla Horváth. 2015. Beading and language class. Introducing the Lylyng Soyum Children Education Centre's attempt to revitalise Ob-Ugric languages and cultures. *Zeszyty Łużyckie*, 48:115–127.

Csilla Horváth. 2016. A manysi örökségnyelv oktatási kísérletei és eredményei. *Általános Nyelvészeti Tanulmányok*, 28:295–306.

Csilla Horváth, Norbert Szilágyi, Ágoston Nagy, and Veronika Vincze. 2017. Language technology resources and tools for Mansi: an overview. In *Proceedings of the Third International Workshop on Computational Linguistics for Uralic Languages*, St. Petersburg, Russia.

Artturi Kannisto. 2013. *Wogulisches Wörterbuch*. Kotimaisten Kielten Keskuksen Julkaisuja, Helsinki.

Tayebeh Mosavi Miangah and Amin Nezarat. 2012. Mobile-Assisted Language Learning. *International Journal of Distributed and Parallel Systems*, 3(1):309–319.

Bernát Munkácsi and Béla Kálmán. 1986. *Wogulisches Wörterbuch*. Akadémiai Kiadó, Budapest.

Evdokija Ivanova Rombandeeva. 2005. *Russko-mansijskij slovar'*. Mirall, Sankt-Peterburg.

Evdokija Ivanova Rombandeeva and Evdokija Aleksandrova Kuzakova. 1982. *Slovar' mansijsko-russkij i russko-mansijskij*. Prosvešenije, Leningrad.

Elena Skribnik and Natalya Koshkaryova. 2006. Khanty and Mansi: the contemporary linguistic situation. In *Shamanism and northern ecology*, pages 207–218, The Hague. Mouton de Gruyter.

Glen Stockwell and Philip Hubbard. 2013. Some emerging principles for mobile-assisted language learning. Technical report, The International Research Foundation for English Language Education, Monterey, CA.

John Traxler. 2005. Defining Mobile Learning. In *IADIS International Conference on Mobile Learning*, pages 261–266, Malta.

Association for Computational Linguistics
209 N. Eighth Street
Stroudsburg, Pennsylvania 18360

ISBN 978-1-7138-0863-3

CURRAN ASSOCIATES INC.
proceedings.com